A SERIOUS DELIRIUM

Michael Allswang

For comments, questions, orders, or permission requests,
please contact the author at: mallswang@orange.fr

For Rachel, Sarah, and Matthieu

CONTENTS

PREFACE

This book of stories was written more or less 40 years ago, then stuck in a drawer while I made a living to support my family. It is an autobiographical fiction, which is an oxymoron, yes, but nonetheless true. That is to say, everything in this book is based on my own experience, sometimes exaggerated, sometimes romanticized, even sometimes pure wishful thinking.

It is also an historical document, an attempt to describe through impressionistic descriptions what it was like to live through the 60's and 70's in the San Francisco Bay Area during the Age of the Hippies.

Finally, and perhaps more importantly for me, this book is an endeavor to try to recapture my state of mind as I lived through a society torn apart by the Vietnam war, the continual American sickness of racism, and the generational divide: a turning point in my life.

STONED SILLY

The Stones are coming! The Stones are coming! The cry went up all over the Bay Area. Woodstock West it was gonna be, a free concert, a monstrous love-in. Parents were tearing their hair out, buying handcuffs to keep the kids home; you could hear the screaming and fighting on every block. But all the kids were going. The hippies were comin' down out of the mountains, streaming back to where it started: San Francisco! The roads were filled with hitchhikers from the Mississippi west. Freaks were renting buses, coming up from L.A. Nothing could stop it: they wanted Golden Gate Park but the city fathers panicked, then the racetrack but even the horses got nervous, so it ended up in Altamont out in the boonies. I went with my roommate George and a couple of girls we knew, Marge and Kate. We piled into the car and headed out as the sun rose. We were all in a carnival mood giggling and laughing, passing the joint around, leaving the city by freeway. I felt like ten years old on the Fourth of July.

Soon we were on a little road through rolling brown hills— stopped dead by 80,000 cars. We pulled up onto a hill, got out and walked. The countryside looked like a junk yard, flashes of sunlight off smooth steel. The crowds got thicker as we approached the site; 300,000 laughing, loving, touching, caught up in the feeling. Every ten paces people hawking drugs, all the psychedelics. We decided on mescaline and swallowed it with a smile.

Many had slept the night and were crawling out of bags, pissing in the fields. Others were still inside, making love in the sun. Little kids were everywhere so serious in their playing. We came to a big hollow surrounded by hills, the stage backed up to a speed track. Huge speakers on high towers. No way to get close, but nobody cared. Feeling our way between balloons, bubbles, frisbees and fringes, we found our spot high on a hill....

> *I can't get no satisfaction*
> *I can't get no satisfaction*
> *'Cause I try and I try and I try and I try...*

Hey, brother, pass the joint. Thanks, man, slip me five. Take off my shirt, why not? Wow, look at that girl, taking off all her clothes. Dancing and jiggling, everything's natural, clouds pulsating, the air's vibrating, I swear it. Gotta dance, gotta. Get up, move it, move it, the music movin' me. Talk to people, anybody, say anything, nobody cares. Let it go, let it out, let it rip. Whew! That guy's flippin' out, cryin' and screamin'. Maybe should help him. No, he's got somebody. What goes on in some people's minds? No jive, havin' a baby! Far out! Just feelin' good, feelin' open now. Come here Kate, just a little kiss. That's it. No hang-ups today, nobody's uptight. Pass the wine, George. Hey, grab that joint comin' by! Look, the sky is in front of the clouds, the sky is in the clouds—outta sight!

> *Dying all the time*
> *Lose your dreams and you will lose your mind*
> *And life's unkind...*

Come on, Kate, open up a little more. Yeah, you know how. Dance with me. Come on, more, more. Smile a little. That's it. Love me a little. Okay. Don't cry. It's all right. Everything's all right today. You're beautiful, love. Here, I'm gonna pick you a flower. No, it's not a weed. Today a dandelion is a flower, a sunfl\ower. I'm offering it to you. You're my goddess. I'm at your feet. Anything you want, just smile, be happy—please, please. The past is over, dead. Today, right now, everything's fine. Can't you see it? I don't care if they're killing each other by the stage. That's all right, too. Everything is like it should be. Look at that guy being carried over the crowd like a log. That crazy hat over there. The naked fatties. It's all so marvelous, the colors, the sounds. Don't you feel it? Don't you feel it, Kate? It's the feeling. It spreads from the gut. Stop crying! Everything is marvelous. It has to be. I know it.

> *I want to see you paint it, paint it black,*
> *Black as night, black as coal*
> *I want to see the sun blotted out from the sky...*

Oh, my God. The hills are rolling, really rolling. Getting dizzy. Better sit down. Feel like throwing up. Head aches. Why is George looking at me like that? What did I do? What did I say? Maybe he's jealous 'cause of Kate. Keeps lookin' at me. Must've done somethin' wrong. But what? Always doin' somethin' wrong. Why? What's right, anyway? Beginning to feel suffocated here. All these people. What've I been doing the last hour? Why is everyone lookin' at me? What did I do? Why is everyone judgin' me? Just let me be! Let me be! Leave me alone!...Gotta get outta here. Can't stand it. Stinkin' people judgin' me. Fuckin' George. Gotta run...Hold it, man. Hold it. Steady does it. Nothing's changed. It's all the same. Let the fantasies go. It's just thoughts, you know. Your own thoughts. Nobody's looking at you. Nobody cares. Everybody's stoned. Let it go, man, let it go....George, how you feelin'? You feelin' good? Yeah, man, me too. We'll do that. Sure. A trip to Ensenada, old Mexico. Maybe next week. Sounds good....

> *Come on now together*
> *Get it on together*
> *Everybody together.*

Come on, let's get in a circle. Arms around each other. That's it. No barriers here, no walls between us. We're all together. Nobody cares anymore what anybody thinks, what anybody believes. Look at that lady over there, George, collecting for a cause. People waving her away like she's crazy. Nobody cares now, you know. It's not the time. It's not the place. Only the music has brought us together. The music, George. Electric music. The Stones, Jefferson Airplane, the Dead. We're a new tribe, George, an international tribe. Politics divides, music unites. Sway with the music, George! Unhinge yourself! Unwind yourself! Unscrew yourself! Flow into the music. We're part of a new world I tell you. We're a community without a home. We're a new people wandering over the earth. We're the Electronic Tribe. And today, George, on this glorious day of the gathering of the clans, there can only be peace and love forever. Yes, I know people are being killed up front, I know....

THE THIRD BOOK OF THE LAW

Why I went to the university, I don't know really. It was just something I was expected to do, unwritten, unconscious, in the Jewish blood, I guess. There's a whole other personality there having nothing to do with the self that wants always to be one of the gang, the club member, the frat boy. There is this other self, enjoying study, learning, reading, precision, problem-solving. It exists apart, in the classroom, at my desk at home. They are two personalities that never touch each other, never meet. When I entered the classroom, an invisible inner switch was pulled, my club jacket fell off, my brain became alive. Now that I look back on it, I never talked about my intellectual concerns with anybody. That was for me, and I kept it to myself, as if I was ashamed of it. If any of the guys made fun of my good grades and scholastic honors, rather than being proud I hung my head embarrassed, as if I had committed a sin, a sin against the herd. It was only at home that I could be proud, that I could receive recognition for my intellect with joy. On the other hand, if I came home drunk as a bum, and my father found me the next morning my head in the clothes hamper which I had mistaken for the toilet, my head laying in my own vomit (a mark of great pride for the herd), I had to hang my head again. I had sinned against the Holy Book. He didn't say anything to me, my father, no bawlings out, no deprivals of pocket money, just the slow, silent shaking of the head which meant, 'No hope, no hope for such a boy.'

My grandmother always used to say that one of our ancestors was a Talmudic scholar. How she knew this I do not know, but I am sure it is true, and I am sure as well that a gene or two of his has filtered down to me. I can see him now, a couple of centuries ago, in a poor Jewish village, a *shtetl*, perhaps in Lithuania, perhaps in Russia. He is rocking back and forth in the candlelight in a little wooden room, chanting under his breath. The wife, the little ones, are sleeping in their cots and so do not feel the hunger. For the moment, the rumors of a pogrom to come are forgotten. He is rocking back and forth on the hard bench, *Torah* in hand. It is very dark outside, and he is trying to understand an obscure text in *Leviticus*, the third book of the Law. Before him on the makeshift table is a worn yellow copy of the *Talmud*, the commentary on the *Pentateuch*. Now and then he picks it up, slowly and with reverence, turns to a passage in the *Mishna*, ponders it, weighs it, then goes on to its elaboration in the *Gemara*. He owns no other books. He needs no other books. Everything is here in the Law and the Commentaries. He only has to understand, to understand. He is poor, it is true, very poor. Almost nothing to eat. But when he walks down the street, the wealthy doff their hats to him; when he speaks, they stand in respectful silence; they murmur in agreement as he lets fall a particularly apt quotation. It is he as well that is given the honored place in the synagogue, who is seated at the head of the table; and when a dispute arises among the people, it is to him that they come for advice.

His whole life has been one of learning. At the tender age of three he had entered the *dardeki kheyder*, where from morning to night he swayed and chanted as he went through endless repetitions of strange Hebrew words. He had learned to read there without understanding and to recite the prayers under the lash of the *melamed*. He graduated then to the *khumesh kheyder*, where he had learned to translate as he read, to comprehend. Here, as well, he had begun to read from the Commentaries. A further step was made into the *gemoreh kheyder*. At the age of eight, he had begun there his Talmudic studies in earnest. No more vain repetition by rote, no more learning long passages by heart; now it was interpretation, imagination, understanding. Judged worthy by his teachers and the erudite of the village, he was sent to the *yeshiva,* a rabbinical academy, far away in the town, where he studied, interpreted, and discussed, for seventeen hours a day, the Holy Books of his people. There he honed his mind through long hours of study, intricate and enthusiastic debates, and an open ear to the words of his teachers. After several years he was given no official degree, no formal title, no list of letters after his name. He was a learned man, that was all, that was enough. People called him Rabbi. Now he spends his nights pouring over the same yellow books, always searching, always trying to understand what is beyond understanding. His days are spent in botched attempts to feed his family. Perhaps he is a teacher, perhaps a struggling tradesman. No matter. His thoughts are in the *Torah*, in the *Talmud*, in learning, in trying to understand an obscure passage in *Leviticus*.

As for myself, my real learning began in the toilet. It was *my own idea.* The encyclopedia was in the hallway next to the door, and every time I went I picked up a volume. My idea was to start at "A" and go through "Z", reading five pages a visit. The way I calculated it, I should have been able to finish it in two years if I didn't take any vacations and drank lots of prune juice. I thought I would know everything that way and so prepare myself for life. I was around eight or nine when I had this brilliant idea. It was working very well, too, at least for a couple of weeks, but five pages in an encyclopedia takes quite a long time to read and my parents couldn't understand what I was doing in there so long. Maybe they thought I was sneaking cigarettes or playing with myself or something; I don't know, but they kept asking me what the problem was every time I went to the can. I got sick of the questioning, but didn't want to tell them my idea, so I dropped it and just started reading short articles at random.

I, like my ancestor, went to religious school, too—every Sunday for eight years. Here was another personality cut off from the rest. No gangs here, no intense intellectual stimulation, just a sort of Jewishness I was forced to bathe in. I never understood, though, why I was there. Couldn't figure it out. My parents said I had to go, so I went. A few prayers, a little history, some Hebrew. It had absolutely nothing to do with the rest of my life. I was made to understand that I was part of a people, but nobody explained to me why that was important. At twelve years old you want to know these things. You want to know why. What was religion anyway? Nobody could really explain it all to me. Nobody even tried. Many a Sunday I pretended I was sick. Just didn't see the point of it all. Unlike my ancestor, nothing ever went beyond learning things by rote: prayers, alphabets, customs, holidays, history. I knew it all, but nothing touched me, made me want to be there. Planting trees in Israel, aiding the Jews in Russia—what did that have to do with my life?

It's not quite true that nothing touched me there, stirred something deep, but it wasn't in religious school learning the dates of the Maccabean Revolt. It was in the synagogue during the High Holy Days, on Rosh Hashanah and Yom Kippur, New Year's and the Day of Atonement. I never would have gone, of course, if I hadn't been forced to. It was just too different from the life in the street I was leading where everything was so alive and unpredictable, where a casual smile from a girl in a car could be built in my imagination into the wildest fantasies, where some tough guy looking at me the wrong way could send terror through my bones, where every day my emotions were stirred in a thousand different ways: infatuation, anger, jealousy, fear, joy. Everything was immediately expressed, everything was lived. Sometimes Vikings, Huns, Goths spreading havoc across the neighborhood; sometimes knights, courtiers, troubadours in love with love. But always moving, in motion, engulfed in the savage intensity of raw life. In the religious school learning my lessons, on the contrary, everything was boring and dull and rational, and if I did well it was only because I was supposed to do well. Now and then I would sneak a cigarette in the john just to relieve the smell of "goodness" that permeated everything in the school, for I craved then the thrill of the forbidden. Yet I was touched there, only not in the school, as I said, but on the High Holy Days in the synagogue, on Rosh Hashanah and Yom Kippur, New Year's and the Day of Atonement....

...Walking through huge wooden doors, seemingly made for giants. Women in mink and pearl, the smell of perfume mixed with that of fat Havanas. Low murmur of voices circulating like the sound of blood. The whole family is together for once. Tension, tension, be careful what you say. Secrets to be kept for a thousand years. The happy family, the bold front. I am glad, very glad, we are going into the main sanctuary. Last year it was the chapel with its aluminum, stucco, and balsa. The folding chairs. Who decides who goes where? God, maybe? If so, he had this year pity on our suffering. Here the walls are two feet of stone, the stained glass leaded. Quick, the yarmulkes! The doors closing with murderous finality. Death camp gates. No horns, no sirens, no blasting motorcycles. Sinking into the red pile, in front the lighted menorahs. Why bulbs and not candles? The dark everlasting light: suffering, God eternal, show Thyself! Ooo-ah! Ooo-ah! The shofar, like a bleating lamb, sounds. Rubbing my hand over polished pews,

the purple velvet, ark of gold and silver. Fondling the torn leather prayer book, the page marker of red cloth. Perfume and cigars. Rabbi and cantor appearing, grey, grey hair. Why no beard? Solemnly towards the pulpit adjusting the tallis. Ooo-ah! Ooo-ah!

> Praise be the Lord to whom all praise is due
> Praised be the Lord to whom all praise is due forever
> and ever.

Mean look of the Rabbi to late-comers. Embarrassed scrambling for seats. Long, long passages in Hebrew, the mystery tongue. Rabbi droning, cantor intoning, father chanting under his breath the kaddish over the parents. The old country, the old country! What happened there?! What brought you here?! Chanting and swaying like days of old....the fear, the fear....

> Yis-gad-dal v'yis-kad-dash sh'meh rab-bo...

Cantor rich and baritone, a haunting melody—all the people chant Kol Nidre. I swoon in my seat bathing in the melody, rising and falling, rising and falling like breath. Oh, let me ascend, oh Lord! Above the suffering flesh! Above the cruel torments of my youth! Hands wet with longing, brow feverish with guilt...trailing wisps of perfume and cigars...

> Sh'ma yis-ro-el a-do-nai el-o-hey-nu a-do-nai ech-od.
> Ba-ruch shem k'vod mal-chu-so ley-o-lam va-ed.
> Hear, O Israel: The Lord, our God, the Lord is One.
> Praised be His name whose glorious kingdom is
> forever and ever.

Solemnly, like a heart, the ark is opened. The silver doors, the velvet curtains. A mumbling of prayers. The great scrolls of the Torah lifted up before the people. The pride of the race from the days of Moses, Sinai, Joshua, Canaan. Held up, presented like a bride. The joy of the Law!

Behold, a new doctrine has been given unto you. Forsake it not!

Tinkling of silver ornaments being removed from the handles. The velvet mantle pulled off like a slip of silk. The naked Torah undressed as delicately as one would a virgin....

And it shall come to pass in the end of days, that the mountain of the Lord's house shall be established as the top of the mountains, and shalt be exalted above the hills; and all nations shall flow unto it. And many peoples shall go and say, Come ye, and let us go up to the mountain of the Lord, and the house of the God of Jacob; and He will teach us of His ways, and we will walk in His paths. For out of Zion shall go forth the law, and the word of the Lord from Jerusalem.

Oh, show me the way, dear Lord, show me the way out of the desires of my trembling flesh, the narrow path of righteousness!...The giving of the sermon. About being a Jew, about coming to Temple, about Israel, war, Arabs, Russians, the dangers, the dangers... I lose track of the argument; it passes me by. I don't care. I want more chanting, more Hebrew, more mystery, to be exalted above the hills....

Yiv-ah-rech'cha a-do-nai v'yish-m'rech-ah
Yo-air a-do-nai pa-nav ay-lech-ah vay-hu-nek-ah
Ye-sah a-do-nai pa-nav ay-lech-ah v 'ya-sem l 'cha
sha-lom

Filing out, murmuring, shuffling of feet. Feelings of insignificance. Sage pronouncements on the sermon, compliments to the cantor....Bright sky shimmering, squinting eyes on cement steps descending. "Mazel tov, mazel tov."

Cars, buses, aunts, uncles. More sage pronouncements. Round hats and bald heads. Running off with a cousin looking at girls....The clinging odor of perfume and cigars....

*

The intellectual life, public school, where the written word was God and life was equated with reason. When I think of the hours and hours I spent in front of teachers, teachers whose only vision of education, whose sole mission in life, was to pound into our heads the supreme necessity of the straightness of the right-hand margin and the memorization of facts; in classrooms where every attempt at self-expression was stifled at the root, is it any wonder that the mind, the reasonable thinking mind, became equated with my idea of self.

And I lapped it up like a hungry dog. My fifth-grade teacher used to seat us in files, the ones who got A's on the right, then the B's, the C's, the D's, down to the basket cases on the far left. Of course, we were too young to analyze it at the time, but the silent lesson was that what is "good" is only measured by what is done with the thinking apparatus up in the skull. Like I said, I lapped it up: I had no problem keeping in the A file and I was damned proud of it, too. I figured out early what side of the bread the butter is spread. Besides, Vicki Romensky was in the B file, and if I stayed in the A one, I could usually sit next to her sharing shy glances.

I remember looking often across the room, over at all the F's, the failures, slouched down in their seats, wondering what sort of strange animal they were. They all looked like they were trying to hide or not give a damn. A couple years later I began to hang out with guys like that, the beginning of my life in the street.

It's true, I enjoyed learning, still do. I really don't care what I learn as long as it's something new. In grammar school I was even put in a special class for smart kids. It was filled with weirdos. Barney Cornhusk, for example: he was a nut on electricity—kept making batteries, radios, motors, and stuff. What he liked to do best was make some sort of contraption for giving electric shocks. When he was finally threatened with expulsion for shocking all the girls, he started on amphibians, practically decimating the frog population of the L.A. River. Henry Blainville liked chemistry, especially mixing chemicals that boiled over, changed colors, exploded. All his clothes were covered with acid holes. He looked like a tramp. Myself, I didn't have any particular passion. I was just there because I knew how to please, how to get good grades.

The one thing I really liked about the class, though, was going to the downtown library. It was the first time I went downtown without my parents, and I went all alone. It was like going to China or the moon, a whole new world I knew nothing about. It scared me and attracted me all at once: the drunks, the bums, the derelicts sleeping or dead on the sidewalks, everybody a different color; the jive talk, hand slapping, money and little packets changing hands; the dirty streets, the ugly storefronts, pawnshops, telephone wires, the five and dime where all the teeth in the comb you bought fell out the first time you put it through your hair. I was a tourist of another life and I loved it, especially the smells: the sickening odor of dollar beauty parlors or fries from a greasy spoon; the stench of urine under the overpass or stale wine from a passing drunk. By the time I arrived at the library, after a few rides on the funicular, I could have cared less about the *Life of Reptiles* or *Oliver Twist*. I sat down and read what I liked: *Superman, The Flash, Uncle Scrooge* and *Archie*.

We studied geometry in the class, way before the other kids did. I liked geometry a lot. I liked to go step by step to prove a theorem, make the little diagrams and all. It was so neat and logical; it conformed to my Jewish rationality and love for things of the mind. One thing that bothered me, though, was the axioms. I knew you weren't supposed to question them, but I couldn't help asking myself who the hell this Euclid thought he was making axioms. I mean he was just an old bearded Greek, wasn't he? Now if it was God on a mountain top amidst thunder and lightning who inscribed them in stone, I might have taken them at face value; but this guy Euclid, what did he know anyway that I shouldn't question his all so precious axioms? I mean how did he know if two parallel lines would never meet? Maybe somewhere between Alpha Centauri and the Crab Nebula they *would* meet, and maybe they would even have a nice conversation and a cup of tea. After all, how did he know? How did he know if two perpendicular lines always made a right angle? What if somewhere they made an acute angle, for example, or an obtuse angle, a straight line even, a spiral, an octahedron? Why just a right angle anyway? How boring! Of course, these sorts of questions I always kept to myself. One learns quickly what is expected of one, and the very first rule in geometry was and always will be: *don't question the axioms!*

Don't question the axioms! The byword of the classroom for twenty years. Taking it in and spitting it out. Programmed tighter than a silicon chip in a mainframe computer. *Don't question the axioms!* Just take it in and spit it out, get your grade and forget it. Remember, the better the grade, the better the job; the better the job, the more you make. What else do you need to know anyway? Whatever you do, *don't question the axioms!* If you're studying politics, don't ask why you need parties. If you're studying economics, don't ask why you need money. You get into trouble that way. Just stick to the subject. What's it based on? you ask. Why? you want to know. Don't ask, just don't ask, okay? It's just because and that's it. I told you what's important, what you need to know. The exam's next week, study hard, you'll do all right. Just *don't question the axioms!*

That's how it was, too, that is until the end of my university days, when my rebellious outer life began to make inroads into the inner sanctum of my academic interests. Until then, my life was so compartmentalized, I would sometimes run into myself rioting in the street and not even recognize me. I had all these selves doing all sorts of different things: studying, rioting, chasing women and whatnot, and they never knew each other, were never formally introduced. What I needed was a master of ceremonies to make the proper introductions. I was about as integrated as Birmingham before the sit-ins.

I really had to suffer for it, too. Once I was helping to close down the university over the rights of students to choose their own grades when a big honcho from the university police came up to me on a picket line and asked me my name and student number. I guess they wanted to get me kicked out which would have been a big favor, now that I look back on it; would have saved a lot of time. Instead of the rebel answering him, telling him to go to hell and shove it, or simply giving him what he wanted as the price to pay for what I was doing, I started stammering and blubbering about how I was just on my way to class when I saw a friend in this strange circle in front of the door and started to talk to him; how he had just left to go to the john and wanted me to hold this funny sign for him until he came back. What does it say anyway? "Oh, Off the Pigs. Now what does that mean, officer? Nice day, isn't it? Want a cigarette maybe?," and so on and so forth. Seemed it got all over campus, how I acted. Lost a lot of friends that day, I remember. Must have gone over that a thousand times. Why did I answer him like that? I didn't want to. Couldn't understand it....Just like that phrase in the Bible somebody quoted in class "...for what I would, that do I not; but what I hate, that do I."

As my university life drew to a close, I began, as I said, to take my budding rebellion into the classroom. Not overtly, mind you; it was much too intimate of a setting for me to stick my neck out. No, it took the form of little unorthodox ideas that I would throw into the papers I had learned to spew out on demand like a short-order cook. It was amazing how many pages I could turn out for things that didn't interest me in the least, things like *Incentive and Coercion in Communist China, Jean-Jacques Rousseau: A Study in Psychological Motivations of Political Thought, Prejudice as a Function of Personality and Environment, The Corporate Communities of the Latin American Indian Peasants: Static or Changing?, Great Britain's Relationship to Western Europe: The Recent History, The Common Market, and European Integration, Community and Morality, Skepticism in the Enlightenment, Antigone: A Psychoanalytic Character Analysis, The Impact of National Character Upon American Foreign Policy, The Formation of Cognitions, A Critique of Various Interpretations of Black Violence, Migratory Farm Workers in California,* and on and on.... Now and then, of course, a subject really took hold of me, and I would get a real pleasure in writing it. Such was the case, for example, with *The Artist's Path to Self-Awareness: Tonio Kroger and the Steppenwolf,* or *Anarchism: The Quest for the Absolute.* In many of these papers, though, I managed to throw in my personal revolutionary opinion which usually resulted in marginal notes such as "leap to judgment," or "not substantiated by the evidence presented," and other such nonsense. Thus, the intermingling of my separate selves began with phrases such as these: "It is up to workers themselves to organize in unions and demand, and if necessary, strike, in order to gain decent working and living conditions.", "...a larger fear of alien doctrines and systems which permeates the American mind.", "One would have to be a pacifist to deny the legitimacy of this violence by black people.", "I must create my own moral values based on my awareness of the true nature of justice.", "I stand with Camus in saying that the only truly serious philosophical problem is suicide.", "He must renounce over and over again all those emotional feelings he has with the world until he achieves the ability to laugh at it and all its institutions."

In the world, my burgeoning rebellion began to take on more criminal forms: I began to steal. Not out of necessity—my father was still paying the bills; neither for the simple thrill of it like in junior high when I'd swipe candy bars and bubble gum or go into the department store and put on two pants and three shirts in the dressing room and walk out trying to be nonchalant looking like an overstuffed scarecrow. No, not for that, I stole out of principle, however absurd that may sound. At the time, I was desperately looking for a 'philosophy of life,' but I couldn't come up with anything coherent and rational. It was impossible to simply let my life go on, for it didn't go anywhere except around in circles, thus the necessity, so I thought, of choosing and controlling my actions based on a precise theoretical framework. The problem was that I seemed to always agree with the last person I read as long as their argument was logical and held together, but, of course, everybody's argument was logical and more or less held together—and then I'd start questioning the damn axioms again. First, I decided to be a Marxist until I asked myself how all history can be interpreted in terms of class struggle and economic production when the only thing that seemed to move people that I knew was sex. Then I was going to be an anarchist, not in the sense of anarchy, but in non-coercive institutions and the abolition of the state, but I didn't see how you could put it into practice without wiping out everybody and their greed for money, power, and glory first. Getting increasingly more desperate at my inability to find a philosophy to follow, I decided to explicitly state my positions on various social questions and then begin to put them into practice. Thus it was that the following paper was produced on the subject of theft:

> *To say that a person takes something from someone else without their permission is to state a fact. To say that a person steals something from someone else can never be a fact, only an opinion. It can equally be said that the person has liberated the object from its unrightful owner. The concept of theft is not an absolute; it is socially defined. It is the powers that be which define for the rest of society who is entitled to what. Whether one accepts this distribution of wealth is a matter of choice. I personally do not. Whatever I want I will acquire without any moral scruples. Whether one has a right to an object cannot be legally defined morally, for the law is only the expression of superior power which is never legitimate in itself.*

Trying to be true to my thought, it became a real sin for me to pay for anything, and every time I had to, I always threw the money down on the counter with a wild sneer and an epithet about "capitalist pigs." Needless to say, I was given the strangest looks by the salesgirls. I was going on like this taking everything I could: records, books, pens, cans of spaghetti, tomatoes, shaving cream, pants, underwear, when the inevitable happened and I got caught. It was over a bottle of beer that I carelessly let hang out of my pocket. Of course, I tried to worm my way out of it. What was I going to tell them, that the beer was mine as much as theirs, that the only difference was that the police was on their side? They would never understand the truth, that the only reason the police was on their side was because we slaughtered the Indians, that the beer actually belonged to the tribe that once lived here, but that since they were long since exterminated in the biggest genocide of all, the beer was as much mine as anybody's. You can imagine what they would have thought halfway through such an argument. They would've called for a strait jacket as well. So I tried to get them to buy the old story about putting it in my pocket and forgetting it, which they didn't fall for, but let me go anyway because I must have looked so scared, which I was, so I stopped and looked for another theoretical position to put into practice.

But the whole idea of taking up little positions seemed sort of petty and futile, so I decided rather to simply rebel on the question of the issues of the day, to take my stand with the "movement," which was more or less against the War, against the police, against authority, and for stopping the War, for equal rights, for drugs, rock festivals and the young. But before I could, I had to reason out my position by writing a manifesto which I manifested by putting it in my drawer. I reproduce it here as a historical document that otherwise might be lost to posterity:

A NOTE ON OUR TIMES

"We'll dance on your grave...and on the grave of your pig empire."
—Anita Hoffman

The situation in the United States today is such that a torrent of violence is bound to descend upon the people of this unhappy country. What started out as a movement of spontaneous freedom, love, and cooperation among the youth of the nation has turned, as it had to in its own defense, to a revolutionary politics with all the consequences this implies. Revolution, as has been demonstrated time and again throughout history, has been chosen as the last available alternative of those who have been denied the right to live a decent life—defined as decent by the oppresseds' own values!

Law after law is passed in these times specifically aimed at youth and its culture. The young, in effect, live under a police state: constantly harassed, searched, beaten, jailed, and intimidated. But what is clear in this era is that this generation will not sit by while the powers that control the society attempt to destroy their culture. To try to repress a culture is to strike a person at his most precious point—his dignity as a human being. Human dignity only gains meaning, after all, in relation to a group and person's identification with its culture. That is why so many youths identify with and feel outraged by every act of government which attacks them for their cultural beliefs and practices. Such laws and rules against harmless drugs, rock festivals, long hair, and dissenters—all epitomized in the trial of the Chicago 7—can only lead to a violent hatred of those conducting the attack and of the system which allows it. The response is, and has to be, violence when a group is without effective political power in the society. When this is the case, it is the only tactic which is effective and at the same time brings satisfaction to the participants.

It has reached the point now that youth do not worry about placating this group or that—they know that they are a community and will stand by each other. Those of the older generation (Marx notwithstanding) are essentially the enemy; for they are, in reality, beyond understanding the total commitment to freedom which this generation has acquired. And it is not political freedom we are interested in here, for political freedom is a phantasma anyway, available only to those who have nothing to offer, but a freedom of the mind—a rebellion that says no to all convention and a resounding yes to all new forms and ideas. The older generation attacks precisely for this reason: they have never known freedom and never will and are envious of those who have it. Their attacks are no more than acts of revenge on those youth who say to them, "I am free." To the crusty minds of another generation this takes on the nature of a challenge and their response becomes, "You cannot be free because I am not free," though they scarcely know their own motives.

In the end, it is a war of generations, and I for one will stand with youth and freedom come what may.

After while my rebellion began to take on more bizarre forms. Not being able to rationalize my revolt on theoretical grounds, I began to look at myself with strange feelings of grandeur. I began to tell myself that I was above the needs of common men, that my whim was enough reason to act for a man of my caliber, a man of genius, the artist of the mind that I had to be; and so I wrote again, but now a prose poem on the despair of such a man as I, of such a wise sensitive man that I surely was, whose sole problem was the swamp of mediocrity in which a man of such infinite wisdom was forced by necessity to dwell:

What was it in the development of the Anglo-Saxon culture that tore out of the society that creative life force which gives any meaning to living? How was this abominable pragmatism, this cult of logic, formed into the collective unconscious so as to destroy the elements from which imagination springs? How this pragmatism pulls at those who are elevated, at those who see the irrational as the only reality; how it tries to pull them down to its own mean level of mediocrity! And if the elevated ones are strong (there are not many) and refuse to descend, they are then engulfed by the pragmatic mass culture—at first surrounded, then attacked and praised, beaten and caressed, and finally lost in a sea of nothingness, swept to the abyss down a canyon of despair. The only question left for the elevated man is whether he has cause to hope. Is it ever possible, he asks, to free oneself from this horrible, leech-like mass that sucks the vital life forces from any man who shows a spark of genius? The masses look for new heroes. They look to the elevated man. They should look into themselves.

By reading my masterpiece over and over again, I was thus able to convince myself of its truth and so evade the great fact that apart from getting good grades, I was a thorough incompetent in everything else. After all, wasn't I a Jew, a son of a Jew who was a son of a Jew before that, one of the chosen ones of the land of Israel?

HEADING SOUTH WITH THE BUFFALO

Ever since I left L.A. to go to the university back East for my Master's, I've never wanted to go back. Too many freeways, too much smog, too many bad memories. Now and then, though, I drive down from the City (as San Francisco is called) to see the family. If I have time, I take all day on Route 1 along the coast, enjoying the splendid views over the Pacific. If I feel a bit rushed I take 101 through the hick towns of Santa Maria, Paso Robles, and King City, that is, until Interstate 5 was finished and I'm able to zip down in a few hours through the boring Central Valley, watching the beets grow. This time I drive 5, wanting to get down quick and get it over with— getting more and more anxious the closer I get. My mother will try every which way to get me to stay longer. My father will pressure me to get into the family business. Why did he send me to the university if he wanted me to take over the family store? Can't figure it out. The war between my parents is terrible, leading my mother to drink and my father to the track. The family house is a nice hacienda style in Los Feliz: red tile roof, forged iron railings, even a stained-glass window. So nice on the outside, a living hell inside. Finally, the whole family exploded, my sister and brothers scattered around the world.

After the family dinner with the usual tension, insults, and bickering, the next day I take a drive around the old neighborhood, reliving old memories, absurdly trying to recapture a moment of passion or suffering, when I ran into Johnny Montoya at Winchell's Donuts, the old hangout. It had been a long time since we'd seen each other, over a year ago, a day I won't forget.

We had just graduated from high school then and were cruising around in my Chevy, a couple beers in hand, when we ran into two chicks Johnny knew, Susie Thompson and Nancy Hays. We were both loose at the time and Johnny gave me the high sign to pick them up, letting me know by a certain gesture of the fingers that they were ready for a good time. I pulled up alongside and they got in readily. They'd obviously been drinking and were pretty far gone. Said they wanted to go to Las Vegas. Wanted to know if we'd take them there. Couldn't have been over sixteen, either of them. Sure, why not, but first let's take a little ride, I said. I was pretty excited because if this was the real thing, it was going to be the first time. Mary Wells was on the radio, so I turned it up full blast. I went up to one of the usual spots in the Hollywood Hills overlooking L.A., a place where you can see the lights go on for miles and miles to the sea on a rare day when the smog had lifted. Susie decided she wanted to go at it first with Johnny, so Nancy and I took a walk. When we came back it was my turn with Susie. I was nervous and didn't know quite what to do. Instead of pulling my pants down, I just pulled it out like I was going to take a piss. It was all sort of clumsy-like, me being nervous and she being drunk, but we managed to do it somehow and then it was Nancy's turn. Johnny got firsts again and went in the back seat. Nobody cared about being alone anymore, and Susie and I did what we could up front. It was just at that moment that the fuzz came around the corner. I got scared. This was statutory rape no matter how you looked at it. I stuffed my thing back in, started the car and headed down the hill while they were still going at it in the back seat. The moment I rounded the bend, I zig-zagged through the hills, which I knew like the back of my hand, losing the cops, until I came down to the boulevard. And they were still going at it. What could I do? I turned left and headed back to the neighborhood while they were humping in the back seat like a couple of rabbits, the lights shining, the cars passing. I started cracking up. It just all seemed so damned funny all of a sudden. I laughed so hard, tears were streaming down my cheeks. It began to hurt even in the gut. I couldn't breathe. They finally finished and I was all laughed out just when we arrived at Nancy's house where I told them to get out. They couldn't understand why we weren't going to Vegas. They thought it was all set. They were really disappointed. Susie started to cry. I had to drag them out of the car. I wasn't about to go to Vegas and add kidnapping to the charges. I could already hear the clank of cold steel doors reverberating through long corridors. I found out later that both our names were on the police list of the 30 or so who got into their pants. Luckily, it didn't go any farther, their parents figuring it was better to move than to spread what happened all over town.

I'm glad to see Johnny, even though our lives have gone in different directions. I still love and hate him, still wary of the power he has always possessed over me. After shooting the bull awhile, he invites me over to his place whenever I get the chance.

I do just that the next week. He lives on the East Side, in a little apartment with his girlfriend, a pretty little blonde I've never met before. We sit down on some pillows scattered around the floor. He offers me a drag on his joint which I take and hand back. We just look at each other and don't say anything. I always look to him to take the lead when we're together, so I wait for him to speak—but he doesn't say anything. I don't understand why not. Finally, I get so uncomfortable I ask him how he is. He says all right. He doesn't have to ask me what I've been doing; I told him the other day. He doesn't say anything else. I'm really uncomfortable so I ask him about some of the old gang. He says Don's in jail for stealing a car, Nick's in the navy, and Dick overdosed. I ask him if he's heard from Larry. He just smiles at me. I ask him again. He says he's gone back East to become a lawyer. Then he smiles again. I feel like Dylan's Mr. Jones: something is happening here but I don't know what it is. Then it hits me, it hits me like a knife slicing into my gut! Of course, Larry's a Jew and he's going to become a lawyer, I'm a Jew and I'm going to the university, but Johnny's a Mexican and is fixing cars outside his house! It isn't right! It just isn't right! He's worth more than all of us! He has something in him that none of us have! I'm about to tell him that, tell him that he should go to the university, too, that he can be anything he wants, but at the same time I realize how stupid that would be and wrong that is and how the whole American dream is a fucking lie!

I don't know why I realized that. It must have been the joint, but at that moment I realized that there is no such thing as an American. There are only Jews, Mexicans, Blacks, Italians, Poles, Irish, Germans and whatnot who got thrown together somehow but didn't make anything new at all. So they make the kids say the "Pledge of Allegiance" every day in school to make us be one big happy family. What a crock of shit! We had been so close only a year ago, Johnny and I, and now something bigger than both of us has pulled us apart. I can't understand why it has to be like that; but it's true, it's an indubitable fact: I am a Jew and Johnny is a Mexican and we have nothing to say to each other anymore....

When Johnny buttoned his shirt at the top, we all buttoned our shirts at the top. At the parties we went to, nobody danced until Johnny danced first. He was the leader of our gang in junior high school. He was like a god. Nobody would do anything if he didn't like it. Anything he said, went. It was so important then: to dress right, to talk right, to act right. I couldn't understand this power he had over me—but I liked him, I loved the guy, even though I'd rebel against him all the time. But it never worked. Once during gym, we were playing kickball on opposite teams. The whole idea of kickball, it seemed, was to kick the opposing players in the balls. I was coming down the field and Johnny came up from behind and tripped me up. I went for him with blood in my eyes, swinging wildly. I was ready to kill him if I had to. The coach had to grab me and throw me down. I was out of control. Then we were better friends than ever, though nothing changed: I still did what he wanted. All we used to do together, the gang, was to drink beer and watch fights. Every day after school, it seemed, we'd go to Commonwealth Park and watch a fight being fought over some earth-shaking event like having stepped on somebody's shoes. Then the six-packs and jug wine would come out and we'd guzzle it till we puked, that is, if the cops didn't show up first.

We called ourselves the Kingpins and met once a week after school at a church. We usually called a couple taxis that we piled into. A few blocks away from the church we'd tell the driver to stop and then scatter like chickens without paying. A few minutes later we'd regroup for our meeting....

> *"The meeting of the Kingpins will now come to order."*
>
> *"Bullshit, I'm not ready. I gotta take a piss."*
>
> *"Look, horseface, the meeting is in order. No swearing. You know this is a church, asshole. Okay, Bob, you give the opening invocation."*
>
> *"Bob! You must be kiddin'. He's a devil. You know, he feels up his little sister. He showed me the other day how he does it. He starts off givin' her a lollipop, then pretends he's lookin' for tumors. It's*

disgusting, and you want him to give the invocation!"

"That's bullshit!"

"No swearing, damn it!"

"I don't care. It's not true. We were just playing. We have a nice relationship, that's all. Anyway, you wanted to be the nurse, or don't you remember that, fat mouth."

"Nobody cares if you feel up your sister. Just give the invocation."

"Damn it, I don't feel her up. Dear God, bless this meeting and may we win the football game next Saturday."

"Mike, read the minutes of the last meeting."

"Why does he have to read the minutes? It's a waste of time. We were all here."

"I don't know. This is how they say a meeting's run. Read the fucking minutes."

"Meeting called to order at 3:31 and ten seconds by President Johnny Montoya. Opening invocation given by Steve Birston. Minutes of last meeting read by Mike Allswang. Treasury report given by Donald Frabus. There is $2.13 in the treasury. Dues collected. Talk by church leader on canned food service project. The Kingpins have collected six cans. More effort needed. Talk by Captain Don Born on last week's football game. He said there was not enough team effort, but that the other team won by luck. New members voted on. Henry McDonald voted in. Robert Julian not voted in because he's a

horse's ass. Suggestions were proposed for a new name for the club. They were: Elegants, Aces, Rapiers, Pagans, Jack Knives, Vandals, Strokers, Vatos, Counts, Playboys, Lovers, Gas Bombs, Athlete's Feet, Studs, Longhairs, Fags, Tao-Taos, Pigmies, El Weed Beaters, Alcoholics, El Boys, Emperors, Muchachos, Bads. Upcoming activities at church given by church leader: track meet May 17; movie, The Girl Can't Help It to be shown May 24. Closing invocation by John LeConte. Meeting adjourned at 4:15. Respectfully submitted, Mike Allswang, secretary. Are there any additions or corrections?"

"Yeah, you didn't mention that we voted to jump Bailey after the meeting 'cause he mouthed off."

"Shit, that's not something you put in the minutes."

"Why not, we voted on it, didn't we?"

"Okay, okay, forget it. Frabus, the treasury report."

"Including today's collection, we have $3.44. We'll never get enough money for jerseys at this rate. I move we raise the dues from 10 cents to 25 cents a week."

"I move we lower the dues to 5 cents."

"You would, cheapskate."

"Only one motion at a time. Does anyone second the motion to raise the dues to 25 cents....Nobody. Does anybody second the motion to lower the dues to 5 cents?"

"Second."

"Third."

"Fourth."

"All in favor? Opposed? The motion passed. Our dues are now 5 cents. But everybody brings a dollar next week for jerseys, understand?"

"I want to vote on it."

"Shut up and bring your money, or I'll move you get your ass kicked."

"Don, give the captain's report."

"We won the Gazelles 13 to 0 last week, as you all know. In my opinion we played a shitty game. The only reason we won was because they played even shittier. We've got to work on our pass defense and cut out the arguing in the huddle. When the quarterback gives the play, just go out and do your job. I'm calling a practice Wednesday after school at the playground. If you want to play on Saturday, you'd better be there. And save the beer until after the practice. I don't want any more puking during practice sessions. Also, about the fight after the game. It was stupid and immature. Doug from the church told me to tell you that and that if it happens again we'll be kicked out. Next time we'll have to meet somewhere else to kick ass if they try to mess with us."

"I wanna know why everyone didn't jump in and fight. There are some chickenshits here."

Okay, okay, that's enough. We have to vote on Tom Catlin to see if he's going to be a member. The floor is open for discussion."

"I don't want him in. He's got zits all over his face and he stinks."

"That's no reason. Anyway, he steals his old man's whiskey, and we can get all we want. I want him in. Besides, he said if he gets in we can use his house for our parties. He lives practically in a mansion up in the hills."

"The guy dresses like a fag. He's always got these tight jeans on and he parts his hair in the middle. Shit, I don't want any fags in the club."

"You're full of it. He's no fag. The cat's a stud. He practically falls at the feet of what's her face, the one with the big tits. Besides, he's smart, he gives me all the answers in English."

"Forget it, the guy's lame."

"No, he's a stud, he's all right."

"Any more discussion? No? Okay, all in favor raise your hand. All opposed? Okay, he's in. Who brought him up? Dean? Tell him he's in and bring him next week. And tell him to bring a bottle of whiskey while you're at it. The next order of business is to decide on Larry's initiation hell night after the game next week. The floor is open for discussion."

"What's the floor got to do with it?"

"Shut up, asshole. You're getting a gig for talking out of turn. One swat after the meeting. Now, any suggestions?"

"Bomb him with eggs."

31

"Dowse him with water and honey and roll him on the ground."

"Eat a raw onion."

"Twenty push-ups and ten laps around the field."

"Push a lemon across the field with his nose."

"Shine all our shoes on his knees."

"Anything else? Any objections to any of these? Okay, that's what it'll be then. And as usual he'll be our slave at school for two weeks.'

"Wait, I got another idea. First, you show him a big dog turd, then you blindfold the guy, see; then you tell him to put his hands out and you put a rotten banana in them and tell him to squeeze. Wadda ya think?"

"Yeah, sounds good. We'll add that on, but you bring the dog turd. The next order of business is the party. The first thing is to get a house. Has anybody talked their parents into it yet?"

"Yeah, we can use my pad the Friday after next if there's no drinkin'."

"Forget it!"

"How can we have a party without booze? It's not right."

"Look, it's the only pad we got. We just gotta drink outside, that's all. Besides, Barry lives across from the park. The fuzz won't catch us there."

"How we gonna get the beer?"

"Sing Ho's market. The chink'll sell to anybody, even if you're eight years old. Who'll go? Jerry? Tim? Okay. Let's meet in the park about 7:00. It closes about 6:00. The easiest place to climb the fence is at the corner. That'll give us a good hour to get wasted before going to Barry's. Now we've gotta decide what chicks to invite. Let's hear it, who's goin' with someone? Steve, you want Bev, right? And Dean, you still goin' with Linda? All right. Who else? Dennis, you and Kathy still makin' out behind the gym? Other suggestions?"

"Sandy Champion."

"Champion? She looks like a caveman."

"I don't care. She gives out."

"Shit, you'd take a chimpanzee if it'd let you feel it up."

"Judy Micker."

"Oh, yeah! She's fine, lovely big tits."

"Too bad you'll never see 'em."

"Why not? I've heard from certain people that she likes me."

"Everybody sees you drooling over her. They're just putting you on."

"Well, I talked to her at recess yesterday, and she was very, very friendly, I'll have you know."

"Carol Patson, Carol Patson!"

"God, no! She doesn't even shave her pits."

"I don't care. Yesterday in science we were watchin' a movie, you know, and I put my arm behind me, stretchin', you know, and I touched her leg. And she didn't even move. So I tried it again, you know, and this time I kept my hand there. And she didn't move! I tell ya she didn't move! So I just kept rubbin' her leg through the whole movie, you know. I thought my arm was gonna break. God, I practically came in my pants."

"Okay, Patson. Anyone else?"

"How 'bout Diane, the one with the red hair. She's got a fine bod. Anyone know her?"

"Yeah, she's goin' with some stud in high school. I've seen him. He'd kill ya if ya talked to her. Forget it."

"Everyone keep your eyes open this week and we'll make the final decision at the next meeting. That's all on the agenda. Any other business? No? Okay, Hempel, give the closing invocation."

"Dear God, bless everyone and may we find happiness, beer, and sex at our party."

In high school, jumping into our cars and cruising the boulevards, the Saturday night rite in my '57 Chevy. Sometimes it was Colorado Boulevard in the Valley, sometimes Hollywood Boulevard and the Sunset Strip. Driving around, radio blasting, looking for girls, a party, always a can of beer or a bottle of Bacardi. No plans, nothing to do, just drivin' and drinkin', lookin' for a girl....

"Over there, behind the foreign job, look at that machine!"

"I've seen it, 450 cc's, overhead cam. *Nobody* fucks with him."

"Shit, Jimmy's machine'd wipe him out. Did ya hear what he did at Long Beach in the quarter-mile last Sunday? Shut down Tony Chavez's Impala. Just fucked him over good, blew him all over the strip. Ya shoulda seen it."

"There's a woody with some surfers. Should we hassle 'em?"

"No, man, we don't want hassles tonight, we want chicks."

"Hey, look at that. 'chine fulla five of 'em comin' our way, see 'em?"

"Oh, yeah, say somethin', say somethin'."

"Hey, stop a sec. Don't ya know it's dangerous out here. Those studs in the chopped Buick behind you got rape in their eyes. Maybe ya know where a party is. We'll protect ya goin' over."

"Just bet you will. There is one though, top of the hill up Wilton Avenue."

"So wadda ya doin' here?"

"Well, we just decided to have it. Gotta find some guys."

"Well, you just found some sweetheart, lead the way. We got the beer."

"Nice car you guys got there."

"Just sounds that way. Punched a couple holes in the muffler. I tell ya that case ya wanna drag. You know, it'd be too embarrassing."

"Yeah, okay. Say, you're kinda cute. Just follow us."

"Move it sweetheart, we're right behind you."

"Hey, Mike, turn up the radio. Oh, I love that song. Just makes me wanna grab some chick. Like that one by the rear window. Did you see those boobs? God, I'm already hot."

Then there was the death car. All these big guys gettin' in that old, lowered Ford, and me in the back there, little old me. Just part of the herd lookin' for a fight. This guy standing at the bus stop and Ken starts trying to pick up some chick standing in front of him. The poor slob tries to be gallant, like he's a knight or something, and tells Ken to beat it. "Wanna make me?" Ken says, and the idiot responds, "If I gotta." So Ken jumps out kicking him in the balls and smashing him in the face all in one movement. It was beautiful to watch. I mean from an aesthetic point of view and all. When the guy's head hit the cement, though, I felt really sick to my stomach. It was this dull thud-like sound and he just lay there. I mean nothing moved, not even a twitch. I thought he was dead. I really did. We split real quick. Never knew if the guy lived or died.

Always a fight, everybody lookin' for a fight. I never saw the point of it. Besides, I was scared just all the time. I mean you risked your life every time you went to a high school football game, especially in East L.A. They had knives, you know what I mean, big push-button ones they'd get in Tijuana. Just stick it against you and push the button. Eight inches of steel slipping into my gut just didn't appeal to me for some reason. But you pretend you don't care. I mean you're wearing the uniform: the starched khaki pants flared at the bottom, Sir Guy shirts buttoned at the top, square-toed shoes with a spit shine, the hair long and greasy. You're supposed to be ready when you're dressed like that. It's the uniform of the herd and you do what the herd wants and what the herd wants depends on who's leading the herd, and if he wants to fight you've got to be ready.

Just to be part of the herd you had to go through hell, I mean real hell. It was diabolical what we cooked up for new members when I was a senior and a member of the Tigers. We went and dug a huge pit up in Griffith Park, up in the hills that we knew so well, in some spot that even the deer didn't know about. We dug this pit and one night we got all the initiates, blindfolded them, and took them up after the park closed. Then we stripped them down to their birthday suits and threw them in stark naked. I felt like a member of some demonic sect taking part in a pagan ritual. Like a band of executioners, we stood around the pit in our blue jackets, while the white bodies flickered in the moonlight coming through the trees. Then we swore at them using every name in the book and some that weren't, especially if they had some defect. Marty Davis had a hare lip. We told him to recite the Gettysburg Address, and every time he lisped we let loose with a rotten egg. He got so nervous, he looked like an omelet before he even got started. Then we let go with the rest of the rotting garbage we had taken from the back of restaurants and markets. We lambasted them all with everything we had. They looked like they had been riding inside a garbage truck. Then we poured Tabasco sauce on their balls until it burned, took their clothes and left them there, left them there to get home the best they could, naked in the night. To top it off, we went to the main road in the park, got about twenty big metal trash cans and rolled them down the hill. Enough noise to raise the dead, not to mention the rangers spreading all over the park. A few of the initiates got arrested for indecent exposure. I don't know how they explained the whole thing to their parents. Later we gave them swats with a wooden paddle. We swatted them so hard and so long they had to sit on a pillow for a week. One guy got a vertebra busted. That got us into real hot water with the school, even the police got in on it. Imagine, getting a vertebra busted 'cause he wanted to join the herd....

The big thing was the jackets, fifteen or twenty of us walking down the street, "Tigers" blazoned on our backs. People respected us, or so we thought. Probably just scared out of their wits by fifteen or twenty guys with greasy hair. I thought I was really something, really important. We could do anything and usually did. At least once a week we'd go into some restaurant, just pick one out at random and go in and order everything on the menu. After shoving down two or three hamburgers each, a couple of orders of fries, apple pie and a chocolate shake, we'd just walk out leaving a bill of fifty dollars or so; didn't even leave a tip. For some reason doing that made me giddy as hell; I'd laugh for hours just thinking about it. If we were walking down the street and had nothing better to do, maybe one of us would lean over and snap off an aerial from some jerk's car. So the next guy would do the same. Pretty soon we're snapping them off right and left, like twigs. And then someone else, like Ken, a klepto from age six, would start prying off hubcaps. Half of us would be marching down the boulevard fencing with the aerials screaming "Zorro!" while the rest are sailing the hubcaps back and forth, the first frisbees.

Really felt good just walkin' down the street like that, really good. All of us walkin', jivin', doin' whatever we wanted, just walkin' down the street like that, feelin' strong, feelin' proud. I couldn't understand it, though, when I was by myself I didn't feel like much, didn't feel like much of anything at all, sort of ashamed even to have my jacket on, as if by myself I wouldn't be able to defend the image there of what it represented.

When I didn't have any homework or a steady girl, I only really felt good when I was with the guys. Didn't like being alone at all, it's true. And when I was, I listened to music all the time, preferably soul music and the louder the better. I didn't know who I was unless I had my jacket on. When we all got together, though, I didn't care who I was, never even thought about it, just out for a good time, drinkin' and lovin' and actin' tough. Some of the best times were when we'd all get together, maybe ten of us, with our girls and a couple cases of beer. We'd go on up to the Greek, the outdoor theater in Griffith Park. Not that we'd pay, hell no—we'd all go up in the hills and sneak through an opening in the fence, find a nice soft spot in the brush above the last row of seats and snap open a couple of cans while we mushed it up with our girls. We weren't the only ones either. The kids were all over the place. I didn't realize how many until Belafonte, who was quite an aware guy and didn't care at all if the kids snuck in to hear him sing, until Belafonte, as I say, started in on Matilda. "All those on the left," he'd say. . . . "Matilda, Matilda..." "All those on the right..." "Matilda, Matilda..." After a while, going back and forth like that, he'd pause with a big smile on his face and say, "Now all those up in the hills sing..."And this incredible roar would come pouring down from on high. I mean the kids were everywhere: up in the trees screeching like monkeys, on the light towers dancing, high over the crowd, behind every bush and shrub. It made the paying audience sound like a church choir at a funeral....

*

I wasn't ready to give anybody their due, Caesar or God, but I joined up for six months in the National Guard like a good robot anyway, just to keep from being drafted into the latest war. And God knows I tried to adapt. I really did. I polished my boots so I could even shave in them. I made my bed so tight I could have used it for a trampoline. I even used to like cleaning my rifle, all oily and smooth functioning. But after a while it just got too absurd. I couldn't figure it out. All they wanted me to do was obey. I suppose, when you think about it, that that's sort of normal in the army; but for me it just happened to be where I was, you know, another place to be, like school, where nobody asked me what I thought about anything. I guess I was just getting sick and tired of it. Rebellion was creeping into my nature.

It started out with the notorious letter I received informing me of the high honor being conferred, one of those army letters, with SUBJECT and TO and letters and numbers everywhere that made no sense. I tried everything I could to get out of it but nothing worked. I even sent them a letter from my doctor saying I might die any moment because of my heart. It was a creepy experience when I found out my heart was beating funny. My doc sent me to a specialist who gave me a million tests. I even had to swallow uranium or something while they took X-rays. The specialist didn't say much to me at all. Just listened to my heart, had me run up and down some steps, listened to my heart again, asked me a bunch of dumb questions, took about ten tubes of blood out of me then sent me home. From that he managed to write up a three-page, single-spaced letter to my doctor who just handed it to me without saying a word when I came in. He handed it to me with a very grave expression on his face, as if words would be superfluous at a time like this, as if one of his patients had just kicked the bucket.

The first two pages were taken up with such expressions as "optic fundi normal" and "T3 red cell uptake 14%." I didn't understand most of it, but the gist of the thing was that I was more or less physically okay except for my heart. He even gave me a neurological examination which I wasn't even aware of, or I assumed he must have since one line said that my mental state was "unremarkable," which I started to take offense to until I understood the jargon. It was the last page, though, that made me gulp. After a couple of paragraphs having to do with myocardiums, arrhythmias and T-waves, he says in the same scientific and objective tone: "This is just the situation where young people will suddenly collapse and die and no good reason is found at postmortem." Oh, is that so? How interesting, doctor. You don't say! He goes on: "The reason, however, is becoming increasingly clear that these people are sustaining a cardiac arrhythmia with ectopic beats falling in the hyper-irritable phase of the myocardium, resulting in ventricular fibrillation and their death." Very good, doctor, you are very intelligent. I am glad, very glad, that when I die you will have understood the reason. He continues: "I would classify him as a residual myocarditis with ventricular and atrial irritability, probably secondary to myocardial fibrosis." Thank you, doctor, thank you. A job well done, catalogued, classified, filed, the bill paid. And in conclusion, if it can be believed, he says: "Thank you for allowing me to evaluate this very fascinating problem with you." Well, doctor, if my death can be of service to you and the scientific establishment, and fascinate you in the bargain, then I must say that my life must have been of some use. Thank you, doctor, for this marvelous privilege.

My own physician tried to smooth things over a little by telling me not to worry about it, nobody really knows what may happen, just don't do too much exercise and other such crap, which I didn't really hear because I was stuck on the line "...where young people will suddenly collapse and die...suddenly collapse and die..." I think it was the first time I ever really thought about the possibility of my own death. It really shook me up. It really did. Until then I must have thought I was immortal or something. I never really thought much about my future. Never have. Never seemed to have control over anything anyway, so why worry about it I thought, if I thought about it at all. I did become a little more pensive that week, though. You can't think about your death without thinking about your life, and I began to wonder a little about what the hell I was going to do with it and what it was for. But the army business stopped all that quick enough.

The army doctor just listened to my heart for a second or two and said, "You're all right, nice try, kid." So during the physical, after they took the blood test, I kept squeezing the blood out until I got a few drops into the urine sample. But nothing came of that either. Finally, I asked to see the psychiatrist, and in a very serious tone I told him that "in the past few years my thought processes and lifestyle have increasingly reinforced my belief that I could not function as a responsible member of the armed forces." He didn't go for it, though, not at all. He just gave me this dirty look as if I was a traitor or something and then asked me if I liked boys. I told him I wasn't any fag, but I just couldn't stomach authority any longer. He told me that "that's just what the army is for, my boy, to get you to stomach authority."

While I was taking a Greyhound up to Fort Ord, they were sending my folks a letter that made me puke when I got back six months later. You can always tell a phony letter when it starts out, "Dear Fellow American..." And you can be assured of it when it continues like this:

> *...he is taking his place alongside thousands of other young Americans in the most serious obligation and greatest privilege of citizenship—that of bearing arms for our Country, ready to serve in any emergency....Although his life as an individual will be regulated to acquire the orderly habits needed in group living, you need have no anxiety; this requirement is neither severe nor too demanding. The discipline which we strive to inculcate is simply the cheerful obedience to properly constituted authority....I hope that you will look upon me, the Commander of Fort Ord, as the head of a family. It is a large family, composed of 30,000 busy soldiers.*

I assure you that in carrying out this responsibility,
the moral and spiritual requirements of these young
Americans are fully recognized....

No wonder they never showed us the letter—imagine: 'orderly habits,' 'neither severe nor too demanding,' 'cheerful obedience,' 'head of a family,' 'moral and spiritual requirements.' Do people really believe that stuff when they write it, or do they know it's crap? I'd really like to know that. I really would.

My first two months, basic training, was bearable. The reason it was bearable was because I had this buddy, Ed Bleeker. Ed was a great guy from Missouri or Arkansas or someplace like that, a solid sort of guy. No intellectual, that's for sure, but he knew who he was and what he wanted. What he wanted was to go back to Missouri, or wherever it was, and look for rocks. He had this passion for rocks and wanted to be a geologist. I tried to understand why he had this passion for rocks, but he really couldn't tell me, except that he always liked to collect rocks and label them and put them in little boxes, so he decided he's going to make a career out of it. I thought at the time that it was kind of dumb to make a career out of rocks just because you collected them as a kid. But maybe it wasn't so dumb after all. At least he'd be doing what he likes.

Ed and I were inseparable. All the stupidity and idiocy of army life we turned into jokes we told each other from morning to night. We especially liked to mimic the SDI, sergeant Everly, who reveled in getting us up at 4:00 a.m., have us put on a full pack, and march us ten miles so we could do some rifle practice before breakfast. Here I was again, somebody telling me what to do, and a drunken oaf at that. The only thing he was capable of doing was giving orders and nipping on his bottle of rye. He had this mania for us keeping in step, so whenever I was up front in formation marching down the road, I'd give Ed a wink and get out of step which would get the guy behind me out of step and so on; then Bleeker would do the same in his file and pretty soon we looked like corks bobbing until Sergeant Everly would scream and shout and finally yell, "Double time, march!" which meant we had to run, which wasn't much fun with a full pack, but worth it just the same.

Now and then we'd get a day's leave, just enough time to do the rounds of the bars in Watsonville. You can imagine what sort of place the town is that calls itself "the artichoke capital of the world." It was just as depressing as the base, maybe more so. We'd go into these bars, as I said, where there'd always be three or four hookers waiting for a soldier to come in wanting to get his rocks off, in spite of the saltpeter they put in the food. Most of them were dogs and we usually made it known we weren't interested, but now and then, mostly out of boredom, we'd go upstairs and fool around a bit, which in the end only added to the dreary quality of the place.

All these sergeants screaming at me all the time had me really scared at first, which I suppose was the purpose of it all, "to get you to stomach authority," until I found out the secret: if you slipped them a bottle of whiskey now and then it was amazing the change in attitude that took place. The head cook is a case in point. Until I knew the secret, I had to peel the potatoes, scrub the pots, mop the floor like all the other privates on KP. One night he was wandering through our barracks half-bombed when he offered me a drink in the corridor. We sat down and finished the bottle. The next night he came again, but this time I had gotten myself a bottle of my own, a good bottle of Kentucky bourbon from Jody Hackett who used to sneak them in. When we finished half of it, I gave him the rest which he was really grateful for. I knew he was really grateful because the next time I had KP, the only thing I had to do was put peaches in bowls and pour juice into glasses all day. It was a lesson that served me in good stead in the months to come.

Like I said, the spirit of rebellion was coming to the fore, but it really didn't show itself until after I went home on leave after basic. On leave I attended this marvelous party with all my old friends. It was a marvelous party because I picked up Kathy Kinder whom I took up in the hills where we made love in the car I had borrowed. It was a corvette, and it wasn't easy, but we did it and liked it and said we'd write each other when I went back to the army. Then I caught pneumonia and had to go back to the base with 104° fever. They said I had to go to an army hospital or back to training. Evidently they would have preferred I die than get out of their clutches.

When I got out of the base hospital, I was put in a school to learn how to type all those meaningless letters and numbers you find over all the army correspondence, records, and orders. It was a soft spot and I knew it, and every night I gave thanks to the army clerk in my Guard unit back home, a friend of mine, who got me assigned there instead of some infantry unit where I'd have had to go bang-bang and dig foxholes with the rest of the mercenaries.

Even so, it was boring as hell, and I was really getting fed up with the whole army scene. It all came out one day standing in formation before lunch when one of the guys was playing sergeant for the day. They liked to do that for the suckers who signed up for two or three years, for the ones who showed "leadership potential." They'd let them march us around before lunch a little, to get the "feeling of command," as they put it. Well, this one guy was one of these gung-ho types who decided to give us some sort of lesson on dismounted drill. It was past time for lunch and the platoons were already lined up at the mess hall, which meant we'd be the last ones as it was and,

God, I was hungry. So, I don't know why really, it's something you just don't do, but this guy was just a private like the rest of us and here he was acting like General MacArthur or somebody, so I just blurted out, and pretty loud, too, "Hey, why don't we go to lunch?!" Well, he didn't say anything to me at the time, but the bastard went and squealed to the real sergeant who was a real big mother and mean, too. Just as I was going into eat I got a message to go and see him. He was standing there by the line, and I went up to him and asked him what he wanted. I had an inkling of what it was about, and when I smelled the liquor on his breath, I figured it was all over. Well, I was right. He just started chewing me up and down like I was a rag or a piece of gum. I mean for fifteen minutes he didn't stop going over me from top to bottom, calling me every name in the book and some that weren't. I felt like a plate umpire after a bad call. He was getting beet red and started spitting as he screamed. He even asked if I wanted to fight, that we could go behind the barracks and have it out right then and there. Now I wasn't about to do anything of the sort. He would've demolished me with one swipe of his grimy paw. Besides, I was too damn scared to say a word, not to mention that my knees were shaking so hard that if I tried to walk a step I would have collapsed like a rubber duck. The only thing that saved me from fainting on the spot was this twitch in his lip as he screamed. I just kept focusing on this funny twitch which let the words sort of go by me. Finally, he finished with me and told me to get the hell out of his sight, which I didn't hesitate to do. After that, the only thing that mattered to me was getting out. I bought myself a huge calendar and put it in my locker, and every evening I lit three candles, made seven prostrations, and said a prayer in five different religions before marking off another day with a big black cross.

Then I couldn't stand anything at all. When they put me in an office after I finished the school, the first thing I did was get in a big argument with the clerk over what kind of music we were going to have on the radio. He was from the Middle West and wanted country music. I couldn't stand country music at the time and told him so. I told him I'm from the city and want to hear hard rock and there's no reason I've gotta hear that wailing sentimental shit and that he can shove it up his ass. Of course, that led to heavy words and almost a fight, but eventually we came to some sort of compromise, the point being that I was evidently getting tired of being in the herd, whether of cows, kangaroos, or platoons.

*

After the army however, it still wasn't over, this herd business. When I started going to the university I thought I would join a fraternity because a friend had gotten in and asked me to come in, too. And I did. It was a Jewish fraternity. Why there should be Jewish fraternities and Christian fraternities didn't make sense to me then at all. It was only after about a year that I began to get wise to what was going on, that fraternities had nothing to do with fraternity at all. Naive jerk that I was, I thought it would just be great parties, good friends, and kegs of beer. That was there all right, but it was only the exterior. The whole system was set up from beginning to end for two reasons: get married to a nice Jewish girl and have plenty of ready-made clients after you made it as doctor, dentist, or lawyer. I suppose it would have been all right if I hadn't realized that, I mean just the parties, the beer, the good times would have been enough, but then I felt used. I couldn't understand why we had parties only with the Jewish sororities. It was getting boring. There were a lot more Christian ones and some fine-looking women in them, too. But it never happened.

No one even mentioned it, so ingrained it was in the mentality of the 'brothers' to stick with the Jewish ones.

Another initiation, more slavery. The pledges had to paint the whole damn fraternity house. I did it, though I don't know why. All that work just to join another herd. The 'brothers' really had it in for me, too, because I had let my hair grow after I had got out of the army, long and greasy again like when I was in high school. The only reason I got accepted in the first place was that my older sister's boyfriend was one of the uppity-ups in the hierarchy. I just didn't fit the image at all. They were all 'ivy league' with short hair, button-down collars, and loafers. They called me "greaser" and made fun of how I dressed. But damn it, this time I decided to hold out. Like I said, rebellion was creeping into my nature. I didn't change a thing either and it really bugged them. I presented a bad image to the sororities I was made to understand. When one of the 'brothers' got pinned and we went to the sorority house to serenade them Cyrano-like, they always made sure I was safely in the back out of sight.

The second semester I decided to live in the fraternity house. It was time to leave home, after all, and the thought of living in a pigeonhole in a dormitory left me cold. An apartment would have been okay I suppose, but I didn't have anyone to room with at the time and I didn't like the idea of living alone. My roommate was a guy named Jacob Blumstein, a nice enough guy and lots of laughs. He had no worries at all. Engaged to a nice Jewish girl, after he got his degree he was going into the insurance business with his old man. Every now and then, sort of 'off the cuff,' he would let us know that if we needed any insurance we knew where to go to get the best deal and so forth. Being his roommate, of course, he put a lot more pressure on me to buy his lousy insurance. First it was the car insurance, but that didn't work because I told him my old man pays for my car insurance; then it was theft insurance, but I had nothing to steal. Then he started to work on me for the life insurance: "You know, Mike," he would say, "you never know what's going to happen in this world. You could kick off tomorrow and then what's going to happen to your little loved ones."

"Look, Jake," I answered, "what the hell are you talkin' about. I'm not even married. I don't have any little loved ones. Leave me alone with your fucking insurance!" But we both knew he was just practicing for later, getting the lines down right he copied from his old man.

His great claim to fame, though, was his ability to fart fire. When he decided to put on a show, the word went up and down fraternity row and a great crowd would assemble in the main room. The door would be locked, the lights dimmed, and with great solemnity he would lower his pants. Bending over, he would spread his cheeks and somehow suck in great quantities of air up his ass. Then, striking a match, he would place it next to his butt and let out a tremendous fart that sounded like air coming out of a balloon. The fire blew halfway across the room, and if I had had a more enterprising spirit, I would have brought him to the attention of the army.

There were certain advantages in living in the fraternity house. For example, the midnight porno movies in the basement, all very hush-hush, and the occasional whore brought in to service the thirty or more of us at one shot. Most of the guys were horny as hell waiting to get married to their nice Jewish girls, and by the end of the evening the poor whore was a wobbling wreck.

There was also the file wherein could be found stolen exams for every required course in the university, or copies of term papers from years gone by carefully filed by subject matter.

49

And if someone wanted to run for office at the university, a great help in furthering one's career, everyone was supposed to get out and campaign.

After a year of that I just got sick of the whole goddamn lie and hypocrisy of it all, and with a couple others who felt like me, we moved into an apartment away from the university. I knew something was changing in me because it was about this time that Kennedy got shot. Everybody was so shocked and dumbfounded. Everything closed, everything stopped. People talked in hushed whispers. I couldn't understand it. If you had read a little history, you knew people got assassinated all the time. It didn't do a thing to me. After all, I never knew the guy. Everybody was so glum and sad, it was depressing to be around, so I found an underground movie house that stayed open and I watched some old Laurel and Hardy flicks. It was about this time, too, that I started smoking heavy dope and getting involved in leftist politics, activities definitely frowned upon in fraternity circles. The break was inevitable and I left the frat for good....

*

Sitting in my chair thinking, thinking, thinking...this chair, this refuge, too much effort even to read, just sit and sit and sit. For a whole day without stirring, even for lunch, I sit here. Not like Buddha, no clarity, no void, no crystal vessel of energy; too much thinking, too many thoughts crowding together, confused thoughts, that begin from nowhere and end without resolution.

They come and go, come and go. Like a fly buzzing around your ear. You don't know where it came from, where it's going. It's there, now it's not there, maybe it'll come back, maybe not. You hope it doesn't, it's irritating, but you do nothing to keep it away. Just open a window so it'll fly out, get a newspaper and swat it, can of poison even. No, you do nothing, you just sit here, in fact you begin to wait for it, you begin to miss it, the buzzing, the irritation, the torture of it. It's something after all.

The thoughts come and go, come and go. When there's no thoughts I sit and wait, more exhausted than empty. Sinking down into the chair, the flabby yellow skin sinking further and further. Full of doubt, baffled, perplexed, I rest suspended in the past anchored to my fear. I vegetate, a brother to ferns and grass. Unblinking, I walk through the world, torpid, absent, my face blank, my heart dead. I see nothing. I feel nothing.

Just a member of a herd I was. Now there is no herd, so what does that make me? God, this place is disgusting. How did I end up here, sitting in this filthy chair, thinking and thinking? Everything's at least a whole: my apartment, my job, my mind, my whole life tastes of degeneracy, depravity, gangrene and dry-rot. The lower I sink, it seems, the more I begin to like the smell of the sewers. Where's that depraved poem I wrote the other day? Here, on the floor. Imagine this life inspiring a poem:

> *Where are you my brothers who seek to seek not?*
> *You hide like I in fetid basements and sour rooms,*
> *You climb up mountains of shit*
> *And wipe yourselves with colored maps.*
> *You pee on your battered books;*
> *You shake your cock at the passing owl.*
> *Sometimes I see you spying through the fog—*
> *An instant our pulsing hands we hold—*
> *Then pass on,*
> *Another soul, wandering, wondering:*
> *Does the mist ever give up its moisture to the sea?*

No more head shops around here, no more love-ins and peace rallies, just us derelicts trying to hold on to something that has passed us by. Maybe I should get up before I get bed sores, or rather chair sores. Let's see, I can go to the Paladin on Haight

Street, strike up a conversation with an addict, listen to a long litany of complaints, hates, problems, and diseases. They appreciate someone lending them an ear. I've got nothin' better to do. But then I'd have to put on my shoes. Where are they? Too much trouble. Forget it....The life of the herd. It went on and on, and I became less and less. Now I don't exist at all. I'm a ghost, a phantom, nothing to touch, to feel, just thoughts, the thoughts coming and going, coming and going...

Always thinking, thinking about the herd, the herd that vanished like the buffalo. What do you do when the herd disappears? When you find yourself alone and lean on the dead prairie, when your brother buffalo with pounding hooves drive toward the southern lands to fatten on the green, green grass? What do you do here on the sterile field, where blight spreads like locusts, when you find yourself alone and naked because you made the fatal mistake of asking where the herd was going? Why, it's very simple. No mighty oak do you become, planting deep, deep roots; rather a weeping willow bending and swaying in anguish until you run madly looking for a woman, any woman. And when you find one you fuck away for dear life until you think the only way out of the morass is a good stiff drink. You plunk a fifth of Johnny Walker in front of you and don't stop drinking till it's dry, only to find yourself deeper in the pit. So you stock up on some good heavy pot and smoke so much that you sprout wings, only to fly so high you lose sight of the earth. Or maybe you begin to play some record time after time because it reminds you of some long-forgotten love affair, and like the record, you find your mind going round and round in the same worn groove.

After a few months of it all, the itch begins to mount; the sensuality, the heaviness, the lethargy becomes a sickening deadly weight, and a mania for order takes hold. You begin to plan your day hour by hour, minute by minute, starting with the morning exercises: twenty jumping-jacks, ten push-ups, fifteen squats. Everything is organized down to the last iota. Schedules are written projects are formulated, lists are made—lists of books to read, lists of people to see, lists of places to go—lists, lists, lists. But eventually, of course, none of it comes to pass; you just go on thinking, thinking about the herd....

Family, school, gangs, army, frat, all these different herds, different group lives, that formed me, molded me, made me multiple...for a time...for a time. Am I only that, just an ant in a hill, a fish in a school, a sheep in a flock? Is my whole life just a changing from group to group and without a group am I nothing at all? No, there must be something else in me. I do not know what it is. It has nothing to do with herds at all. It belongs to me, to me alone. It is so small, so little, a deformed dwarf-like thing. It only watches, watches the herds send me spinning through life. I feel it here when I sit alone in my chair. It is me, a real me. It does not exist out there in life. It can only watch the herd-selves act: all my idiocies. It knows, it knows, but has no strength, no power. It never acts. Who am I, then? Who am I?

GEORGE

George is a funny-looking guy. He has long, stringy red hair and moles all over his body thin as a stick. He's only about twenty-three, but whenever I look at him I'm always struck by his protruding chin with its perpetual red stubble: it's the chin of an old man, and it doesn't go at all with his childlike delft-blue eyes. I suppose the incongruity of his features is made even more evident when he speaks, for he has this high, shrill voice that causes people to look at each other with knowing sidelong glances. The fluorescent-colored pants he always wears only confirms the underlying impression, but George is anything but gay. I've never seen a guy more highly sexed, and it's always directed on the opposite number. George would be the first to admit that he isn't very discriminatory; he has just separated from his wife, it's true, yet I often wonder how he crawls into bed with some of the girls he picks up on the street.

I met George a couple of years before we moved in together. I met him in a bar in North Beach and we hit it off from the start. I liked him because he was crazy and didn't seem to give a shit. He didn't know what the word 'no' meant, and I needed people like that around me. I was just beginning my own initiation rite into the world, and I was in want of any help I could get.

While those who come over call our underground apartment disgusting, it seems to fit our lives. The living room, for example, the size of a closet in any normal apartment, doubling as George's bedroom, is as well an ingenious compromise between a study and an opium den. Reader that I am, I insisted on a comfortable place to read and a place to put my books in orderly fashion. George, who could have cared less, was primarily interested in the right atmosphere for seducing the women he would bring home from his forays in the City. We were both agreed, however, on the need for a place to smoke serenely the fine kilo of Columbian grass we had studiously procured when we moved in at least a month before we made the effort to find stove and refrigerator at St. Vincent de Paul's. We solved the problem through a lighting technique that would have made any stagehand proud. For my pleasure, the books were stacked around the walls in brick-and-shelf bookcases, the materials filched at night from a neighborhood construction project, while an overstuffed chair we found at the Alameda flea market was put in one corner with a 100-watt floor lamp beside. For George, his mattress was strewn on the floor in the corner, next to which we placed a small table lamp fitted with a little red bulb. Around the wall for getting stoned we pasted fluorescent psychedelic posters and strung Christmas tree lights, all a deep yellow, so that the bulbs rested squarely in the center of each poster. Depending on the activity—reading, fucking, or smoking—it was a simple matter of turning on the appropriate lights.

When George walks into the apartment it's like an electro-magnetic charge in the atmosphere. He's hung up on so many problems that when he sits down they all rush at him like bulls causing him to spring away like a capeless matador. Up and down, pacing, twitching about, I'm unable to think, read or even listen to music. George's presence is pure activity: always talking, fidgeting, chain-smoking like a fiend. He doesn't analyze his problems much, just ignores them through action, primarily lovemaking. He makes his living student-teaching photography in some high school in the suburbs, a job which causes him no end of anguish. It's not the photography, no, but the not so little sixteen-year-olds he's dying to get into. I don't think he's taken one photograph the whole year we've been living together, and I must have asked him a thousand times why he's teaching what he should be doing, for there is no doubt he's a hell of a photographer. He specializes in nudes, female, in particular his wife. His photos always have this art nouveau quality about them, ethereal, even the trees seem to float. To enhance the nebulous atmosphere, he often drapes Sylvia in gauze or some other diaphanous fabric that he rips off from the Emporium, the big department store in the City. Sylvia's body only adds to the effect. You would think you were looking at some anatomical diagram of the circulatory system, such is her skin translucent, and she always wears her hair up in tufts and wisps so that when her back is to the light you would swear she was blessed with the Virgin's aureole. Whatever the fashion of the moment, she's always wearing a long, lacy, organdy dress, often sheer from the waist up, and, of course, like all the girls in San Francisco, she never wears a bra.

They liked to go up in the foothills above Oakland, where there are strong raw forests and splendid backdrops of the Bay. George has recounted to me often, not without a little wistfulness, how after a few hours of picture-taking, they would find a secluded glade and make love until sunset when they would watch the sun fall behind the Golden Gate Bridge, leaving the Bay in a brilliant array of silvery-red streaks.

Now he doesn't see her much except to arrange the divorce and see who she is sleeping with, for despite himself he is still insanely jealous. When he found out she's been shacking up with a black from Hunter's Point, he became worse than the nervous wreck he usually is, scratching at the walls like a caged cougar, screaming over and over, "That fuckin' bitch!

That fuckin' bitch!" until finally he jumps into his Ford and spins over the freeways half the night working it off. There is still that racist streak in him he hasn't yet gouged out of his middle-American soul.

But as I say, they have recently separated. They are childhood sweethearts from a small town in Indiana, and from what I gather from our conversations, for there are certain things that George won't talk about, she's part of a past he wants to leave and forget. George is an artist who hasn't yet accepted his destiny, a creator still enmeshed in the nightmare of the past. It seems so strange the way he goes off in the morning to teach after a night together smoking dope, hitting bars. Sometimes, after he leaves in the morning, a bleary-eyed girl that I vaguely remember from the night before might come straggling out of his room, and if I am alone myself and not working, we'll spend the rest of the day in bed. Often we're still there when he comes back and all three of us will pass an indescribable night together, George never forgetting to set the alarm for his morning class the next day.

One night Sylvia comes over to sign some legal papers just as I am about to slip into the shower. In one of my rare good moods, I jokingly suggest we all climb in the little cubicle together for a mutual washing. Much to my amazement, they both agree. George isn't at all jealous, I suppose because he's there, that he knows I don't care one way or another. Not that I am oblivious to obvious charms, but up till now Sylvia has been no more than George's wife, separated, true, but silently understood, untouchable. As for Sylvia, she is passive, pensive, doesn't talk much, but in her quiet way does what comes naturally. We all undress in feverish anticipation.

After fumbling like drunken funambulists with the knobs, our aroused flesh is quickly pinked by a hot steady stream and we both begin lathering up Sylvia's luscious dewberry body, me behind starting with the neck smooth as a baby's thigh, down over the back gently tapering, lingering long over the buttocks, kneading the opulent globes, now and then slipping a finger up between her legs producing short squealy squeaks. George meanwhile is shaking like a waif, mouth over breast, massaging loin and flank, her hand coiling his bolt like a rusted nut. After a couple of minutes like this I can't take it any more at all, and I spin her around trying to lift her up, around and in all at once, but what with the soap and the strangled space, we keep sliding all over each other, George hopping up and down shouting "Yes! Yes! Hurry! Hurry!" trying to help, pulling around a leg or picking up a handful. And then somehow slipping on one of the soaps, I fall with Sylvia on top of me and George sprawled over the two of us, and we just lay there like maniacs screeching and shaking, the hot sheets of water pinning us, Sylvia managing finally to get an arm up to turn off the taps screaming, "You're both insane! Let's go into the other room or we'll never get it on!"

The etiquette of the situation is obvious, and with a gracious "Husbands first..." I bow away, though actually more excited at owling them than getting my end in, a spectacle infinitely more arousing than the crude porno movies on Market Street I sometimes frequent in my more morbid moods.

George doesn't waste any time in preliminaries, for Sylvia is still evidently flushed and juicy. I quickly see why he has no problem getting women. Often he boasts of his sexual prowess, how he has trained himself like a seal to pump away for forty-five minutes to an hour without coming. "I'm a real butter churn," he likes to say. I take it all with a grain of salt, but now I see he is scarcely exaggerating. Really a marvelous technique: they change rhythms, positions, sometimes drifting but never withdrawing, knowing instinctively what the other likes and wants, so used to each other they are that their undulations just go on and on endlessly like smooth-running synchromesh.

I stare at them agape, enthralled like a child at the circus—two writhing contortionists in the main arena. Then standing over this pulsating protoplasm, in the honey-colored light of the decrepit room, they merge under my frozen gaze, for an evanescent instant, into what I imagine is an androgynous Hindu god....

A second later, however, I'm on all fours, crawling to observe from every angle—front, back, side—getting more and more eager, hard as a bar, now and then suggesting a new position or stroking some flesh that I don't care is whose. I can see now they are just at it for the physical pleasure, their bitter mixture of unspoken hostility and fear of separation doesn't leave any room for tenderness—which, from my point of view, only makes it easier to take my turn. When the orgasmic spasm finally arrives, the screeching and wailing has more the air of a medieval torture chamber than the convulsive release that poets like to call the 'moment of infinity.'

Looking in Sylvia's vitreous eyes, a pillowy regard beckons me, and like a padlock we clamp together, me heedless that I might be incapable of measuring up to George's sexual wizardry. I try to hold back as long as possible, but already taut beyond endurance, I soon shoot my wad while Sylvia lets loose with a torrent of unintelligible broken stutterings, upper lip turned under, eyes spinning in their sockets like a slot machine gone screwy.

*

One day George suggests we take a trip to the Geysers and being ready for anything that involves a change of scenery, I'm all for it. Not that George will tell me what it's all about; oh no, just that it's some sort of health spa hidden up in the hills north of Santa Rosa, near Geyserville. "It'll release your tensions," he says with a mysterious smile, and when I pump him for more information, all he does is blink and rub his crotch. We make the date for Saturday after next. When the day arrives I am so depressed after my week working as an indentured servant, I'm sure I would spend the whole weekend on my back if George didn't pull me out of bed, dress me and brush my teeth. Drinking our coffee, I ask him if I'll need my bathing suit, but he just shakes his head with a stupid grin on his face, eyes gleaming.

It's early morning before the fog lifts as we roll through the sleeping beauty of San Francisco, then across the Bay Bridge where, looking back through the haze, the City is like a motionless crab, the piers grasping at the Bay, the first glimmerings of sunlight piercing off the high protuberances of its steel-glass shell. Below, the soup is churning up briny vapors that drift through the web of girders, cables, beams, and pipes through which we are traveling like heedless flies. On reaching the end of the bridge, we glide with the traffic onto the freeway northbound, skirting the Bay. The fog has begun to lift here, and on the beach between the freeway and the water can be seen those abstract driftwood sculptures still damp and glistening in the morning light. Looking like scarecrows or sometimes like a menagerie of animals from the Land of Oz, they often seem to move as I go by. They were there when I came to the Bay Area and there they still stand. I don't know why, but there is something mysterious about them there on the tidal flats. Who built them? How long have they been there? One good storm and they would all be kindling, but for me they are as perennial as the megaliths of Carnac or the great stone heads of Easter Island.

"George," I say as they fade out of sight, "why don't we stop at the Berkeley Pier. We've got plenty of time and, you know, to see the Bay at sunrise from the end of the dock..."

"Sure, good idea," he answers in an unusually cheerful mood, "and perhaps we'll find some little robin red breast, a little female early bird looking for my worm." With this, he makes a beautiful four-lane crossing to reach the exit, cutting off two pickups and a motorcycle. The screeching of brakes goes right up my spine, but the crash never comes....

There isn't a soul to be seen when we arrive, and as we walk down the quarter mile of pier stretching out into the Bay, the morning silence is only broken by the overhead caw of soaring gulls. I often come here by myself to meditate, to muse at the end where the pier has been cleaved for the passage of boats, at the end where not many care to walk. Here, standing on the wooden planks with the water lapping against the pilings, the Bay encircled by the surrounding hills, the islands Angel, Alcatraz, Yerba Buena, surrounded in their turn by the waters of the Bay, San Francisco farther away jutting up from the earth like a proud breast, the ships passing under the Bay Bridge or through the Golden Gate into the open sea; here I renew myself, gather my strength, make my plans. It is my sacred spot and I feel a little uneasy coming here with someone else, even George. Perhaps, I think, I might be offending my gods, but he seems to sense my reverence for the place and desists from his usual crude pleasantries.

When we can walk no further, the both of us lean on the railing and take in the panorama that seems to have been created for us alone. The Bay seems more beautiful this morning than ever before. Perhaps being here with a friend adds to the feeling of brotherhood, of connection, for I feel very close to George now, more than any other time before or since; and I feel, too, the joy of this morning view overwhelming all my problems at this one moment. Observing the first rays of the rising sun imbuing the haze with a warm orange glow and the still water, smooth and apprehensive; hearing a silence only broken by the deep bass tone of a foghorn from an unseen ship; the moon barely visible and fading quickly against the brightening light of day—at this moment, what else can really matter? How small I begin to feel! How puny! A drop of dew could drown me now! Not a thought disturbs my gaze, no question demands a response—and then within this void at the very bottom of the hollow that I have become, an ember glows and rises and bursts into flame! My trunk an alembic, a vessel for the flowing philter of fire, a light force expanding in my abdomen like hot balloons rising in white-blue sky. I will or cannot move; a living statue, not of salt but of fire, standing here radiating pure energy-essence of the interior of stars....

"Strange," George says breaking the silence, "how the pier goes on after the break. It seems so unreal. There must be another quarter mile of it sitting out there useless."

"Yeah, I know what you mean," I hear myself say, "It attracts you somehow, doesn't it? I mean to get past the break without getting wet. I know it's impossible, yet after standing here awhile, sometimes I want so badly to get over there that I almost think I can fly to it if I try hard enough. Once I actually had to stop myself from climbing up on the railing."

"Look, I'm getting spooked. Let's split and get up to the Geysers before we forget what we started out for."

'Started out for?' I think. I don't know what we started out for, with him keeping the whole thing such a big secret. But I like it. It appeals to my sense of adventure. Having no expectations, everything is possible, everything is new....

Oozing contentment, we are soon heading north again through Martinez, by the huge rusting tanks filled with oil for America's creaky machinery, past Petaluma into undulating farmland bellying against distant mountain peaks.

"What are you gonna do next year, George?" I ask as we speed through the beet fields.

"I dunno. Try to get a job teachin' photography, I suppose. In fact, if things stay the same, I'll be able to keep the job I've got now."

"I don't understand you. Why don't you try to make money taking photographs instead of teaching other people how to do it? You're good, you could sell your stuff. I know you'd rather be a photographer than a teacher."

"That's right, but I've gotta make money too, and at least this way I'm still keeping my hand in."

"From what I see, the only thing you want to keep your hand in is the pants of those budding girl students of yours. You haven't even set up your darkroom yet. And don't tell me about the cockroaches; we can get rid of 'em. You know, you're just compromising your whole life away, wasting your time. I hate to say it, George, but what you're living is a lie."

"Well, just look who the hell is talking! You keep moaning you want to be a writer. The only thing I've ever seen is one idiotic line you were so proud of you kept shouting it to me for a week. How did it go now? Something about moons of faraway planets revolving around a pig's entrails or something like that. Jesus Christ! You're the one to talk! Workin' in a fuckin' bakery! At least if you're not going to write, you could get a job teaching, too. I mean, after all, what did you spend five years in the university for anyway, with a master's degree to boot!"

I don't answer him. What's the use? What more can I say? These conversations always come down to the same thing: what right do you have to say anything if you're not doing something 'useful'—translate that to mean 'making good money.' As if thinking is not doing something useful, as if money had anything to do with it at all.

In any case, it can't be much farther now. We're getting higher and the land more savage. The car twists and turns through the narrow passage carved out of the mountains by the river still coursing the opposite way below us, separated from the road by a steep bank.

Why, I begin to ask myself, is it that nobody thinks like me? Am I really that strange? Why am I so sure that what I know is true? Maybe it's all a dream. Maybe they're right, maybe when you die, at the gates of Heaven, Saint Peter only asks you how much money you made. All those who made over a million are on the right hand of God, anything less and there's gnashing of teeth. But it seems so insane to me to decide what you do with your life because you've got a friend in the business, to decide your whole life on one throw of the dice. You've got to get out in the world, it seems to me, get shaken up, tumbled about, until everything becomes a jumble, chaos, and you're even a little crazy—until one day you find out who you are, the picture comes back into focus, only it's not the same one you left behind in school or with family and friends. But you don't know it until you go back. Then paranoia sets in and false confusion because people treat you like you were and not like you are, or think you are, and you begin to ask yourself exactly who is right, you or them? For they seem to be unanimous and you're only one; and so you begin to read: Nietzsche, Camus, Saint John, Lao Tsu, Krishnamurti, Dostoevsky, Sartre, the I Ching, Kafka, Bergson, Plato, the Bhagavat Gita, Marcuse and all the rest, but that only brings you further and further into

64

yourself and you go down like Narcissus looking into the pool, and pretty soon you go so far that you don't know how to get back up and you just wander around like a zombie at the bottom and you don't know where reality is; so you look for it everywhere: in goldfish, rubber bands, old book covers, tin cans; you talk to the trees, your only friends are the birds, you fight against the wind and play tag with the tide; and if you don't crack up or get sick or get hooked on drugs, you might be lucky enough to find a woman to take refuge in, and perhaps she'll be strong enough to keep you afloat until you're put back together again, until you plant some roots to replace the microscopic strands that were ripped away, something to grow your soul on, planted in the earth and reaching toward the stars. Can't they understand that something new must be created—and from scratch! Otherwise I'm nothing, just somebody else's mind, somebody else's tool; I wouldn't be me, or what I could be, if I don't give up, if I just hang on—but maybe they're right, maybe it's just an escape all this, a fear of the world; maybe it's true, that all we are is our job, our weekly paycheck. But then why do I feel so false at my job, as though I'm not being true to myself? But then what is myself?

So confusing, were the times always like this? Was work always to do violence to something inside one? Perhaps there was a golden age once upon a time: the reverent pilgrim kneeling humbly before the shrine, the peasant with his singing scythe cutting the great stalks of wheat, the goldsmith fondling his precious tools, the firmament enclosing the world; no relativity, no uncertainty principle, no class struggle, no theories about living at all, just life to be lived—eat, drink and be merry—where work was part of your life like the heart or the liver, not something to be undergone to prove you're a man and then escape from like the plague. Time goes on, events succeed one another, and it doesn't seem like progress at all, only regression leading to the final catastrophe.

Going to the Geysers, what for?... More sex and drugs, no doubt....God, is this what it's all about? ...This is life?...Some lousy job, then sex and drugs....

"George," I say in order, no doubt, to make myself believe I'm still in the world, "maybe the only solution is to commit suicide. People are considered heroes who die for their country, no? But how easy that is, to do what is expected of you. The most courageous feat of all, it seems to me, would be to die alone in revolt, not out of despair but out of lucidity. Like the writer who refuses to write, knowing he can never really express in words what he has experienced; to take this up to the level of life itself, to refuse to live because one's life can never express the feeling, perhaps a vision once touched, of what a life could be."

"What? Kill yourself because you can't be perfect?! If that's the case, you should've done yourself in ten times over, considering the life you're leading. Why don't you kill yourself if you believe the world is such a rotten mess, which, if I might add, really means that it sullies your lily-white spirit, right?"

"Why not, indeed! Logically, there's no reason not to. Life is absurd, right? Sometimes, you know, I really am desperate; I really do think about suicide, at least to the point of saying to myself that if nothing else eases the suffering, I still have that as a last resort. But it's usually at these moments, when I'm completely without any hope at all that something flickers inside me. I don't understand it in the least. I'm at the breaking point of despair and misery when this feeling just comes on, so marvelous and liberating, that I can't help believing that there is something about life that my thought can never comprehend. It's almost like a power within me that could change worlds;

and so I spend my time trying to find this feeling again. I don't even know what is real anymore, George. Am I supposed to deny my own experiences because everyone says I'm not facing reality? Do I have to have the same reality as everybody else? Do I? The trouble is the feeling never lasts, and the more I try to keep it, the faster it disappears. Why is that? I feel so marvelous, God-like, and then it all goes away leaving me with this horrible reality of everyday life which is absolutely without any meaning at all to me. And yet everyone else is in this life and I ask myself what they are doing here. How can they live in this absurdity? And yet, I too have to live here—I don't know, I guess I'm just not ready. I must have fallen out of my nest before I learned to fly. I want to be God and haven't even become a man, a skeleton with wings if you know what I mean. It just isn't easy to break with ideas, values, ambitions that you've been carrying around for years not even knowing where they've come from; but now, since I've fallen off the merry-go-round, all this so-called culture surrounding us— schools, newspapers, television, publicity, movies, Disneylands, books spilling out into the streets—it's like a huge plot concocted somewhere to keep us from life."

George just looks at me and, with a disgusted weary sigh, says, "The Geysers, I'm going to the Geysers...."

We travel on in silence, the curving road now slicing through forest of pine. All I can think of is how my life has become such a rotten mess. Money! How do you wrest it from society without spraining your life over a job? Society for me is like a fortress. I have no idea how to make my way in. All I want is to travel through life like a man on the road, to travel as lyrically as a clear running brook, as a chimpanzee swinging, a deer running through thick forest, neither flood nor drought, never a misstep, inaudible movement in lucid tranquility. But what lay ahead of me now? All I can think of is that I will be slowly dying in a bakery the rest of my life packing macaroons. What's the difference what job I have, now that the veil has fallen, now that the world has become a dark and cavernous place.

What, indeed, lay ahead of me now, for this chameleon slithering on the suburbs of humanity? Once I had the comfort of my family, the laughter of my friends. Books by the score, music by the hour, a woman's kiss occupied my brain and heart. But now, without need of pacifiers nor distractions, when my desire becomes too great, I simply gnaw on my knuckles until they bleed. I, who have traveled over oceans of love, continents of anguish, mountains of ecstasy and valleys of despair; I, who have known every human emotion to its bitter extreme and have now been prematurely aborted as a fetus smothered in placenta and crushed chrysalis, I still dream dreams of which even a child would be ashamed. I search for the mystic deliria in every object—in matchbooks, trees, dogs, toads, and coffee cups. I wait weeks to hear the Word. Often it comes as only a slight whisper from below: "You know, young man, it's all folly. Go get a job. Get to work. Make some money." And I tried, but a career was denied me. I tried to climb high brick walls that only grew higher with each attempt. I dug tunnels and found only floods. I took long tortuous routes only to end up lost and alone. I began to travel in circles like a top, spinning webs of Chinese tapestry, African masks, and starry lace. I created worlds of unknown splendor out of emotions from an unheard-of ecstasy. I saw temples tentaculiform crackling across a lacustrine sky, columns of majolica, altars of aquamanilia, soaring behind the flaming jets of battling rocket ships. As I stepped into the endoplasmic warp, on liquid streets below undulating skies, under the spell of galactic rhythms, I entered stealthily the realm of reality. Here the clouds congealed, the moon dispersed, and the mandragora leaves were tinctured with silvery floss. From the human paludal swamp where I often descended, as from Venus, arose the ophidian cadenzas, planting on my sex their venomous fangs. But like a geyser I would rise again, heedless, balancing on a mystic drop, peering through the veil, renascent, dissolving in the apogee of my impalpable vision! And I drank the sacred juice of the gods, I danced alone like a Greek, I kissed the lips of the Abominable Whore and raped the nun in her convent. I burned under the dunes of the body of Woman and shivered alone on the sea. Now, having savored the lemon of bitterness and frozen on the glacier of hope, having sucked dry the rhymes of ancient mariners and breasts of mother-of-pearl, what, I ask, is left for this pale ash whose sole activity is in the horrible tedium of watching the growth of a rose? Is there no escape? Am I doomed to this life? Snuffed out already, crushed like a worm after only a first feeble glow? Oh,. my God! Am I trapped forever?! What am I to do, to do?!

"Let me out!" I scream, "Let me out!"

"Whaaaaaat?"

"Stop the fuckin' car, damn it! I gotta get out!"

"Okay, okay, take it easy," and he pulls over to the side overlooking the river.

In a panic I jump out of the car and run to where I can look down at the current. Kaleidoscopic flecks of sun reflect off the writhing water. A fisherman in hip boots stands in the river to the right. Immediately I launch myself, half falling, half sliding down the bank. When I reach bottom, almost in a frenzy, without knowing why, I pull out pen and notepad and begin to write....

After a time, in a trance, I read what has been written, wondering where the words came from. Some, I know, I'll have to look up in the dictionary....

Feeling weary, my eyes wander from the paper, gaze haphazardly over the landscape, and, as if fixed on a beam, climb far above the horizon, up high towards the late-morning sun: a shimmering ball in white sky, dilating and contracting like a motionless fish breathing in hot sea depths. The perspiration is trickling down over my forehead; my eyes burn from the glare and the salt. My shirt is clingy on my sweat-soaked body, and I sink back into the long thick grass heavy with dew. As I watch a swallow swoop overhead, a pebble drumrolls down the bank, ringing into the water with the clear note of a bell. The dazzling sky-brightness soon infuses my commingling senses with a warm stupor, setting me afloat, a child drifting among the reeds....Drowsy, a whooshing, whip-like sound startles me into awareness, and my eyes open onto a fishing line spiraling gracefully, looping from a long distance into the river. I follow the hook as it breaks through the surface and watch it sink in the slow-moving waters liquescent and clear. Soon a trout with shuddering, silvery-red fins wriggles close to the suspended worm. It bites, but then I lose it amid the frothy river and the swaying plants. When I again find the trout inching back upstream, reeled in by the old fisherman, my eye catches a thick straight branch being carried in the opposite direction. I follow it passing by me, swept by the current creaming slow and dense around scattered boulders. It is cradled gently in the midstream flow, descending far from the grassy banks, until it vanishes unswerving around a bend. Only the sure monotonous current remains now, yet I continue to gaze far, far off, on this vein nourishing from the mountain the land to the sea....

"Hey, come on! Let's go! The Geysers, remember!"

George's voice seems to come from far away, underground. I raise myself slowly as the joy mounts in my chest.

"Yes, of course, of course!" I scream as I scramble back up the bank.

As I get back into the car I respond to George's quizzical look with a strange smile.

"How long did you say it was before we reach the Geysers?" I ask.

Chattering the rest of the way, mostly about George's latest sexual exploits, we soon approach what he says is the Geysers, but all I can see are huge pumping stations ringing the valley to capture the underground steam, funnel it through whirring turbines, and transform it into electricity buzzing through wires to the cities in the plain.

"I thought you said this was some sort of resort," I say. "It's beginning to look more like Pittsburgh to me."

"Hold on, when we get into the valley, you won't see the machinery, and even if you could you wouldn't notice—you'll have other things on your mind, believe me!"

*

We pull up in front of a weather-beaten cafe, a wormy wooden building that looks as if it came from one of the ghost towns in the gold rush country. A crooked sign over the door reads 'Ed's Eatery' in faded red letters.

"Come on," George says, "Let's get a bite to eat. I'm starved, and besides, you might forget to eat the next couple days. Ed here runs the whole place, a crazy old coot who wanted to create a Garden of Eden for us children of Satan. Everything's cheap as hell 'cause he knows he's gonna make a fortune when the electric company buys him out."

Inside, the place is half-filled with people at the tables or counter in various stages of undress: guys without shirts or just in bathing suits, girls in kimonos and bikinis with arms akimbo, or just long T-shirts with evidently nothing else at all. Hardly anybody is talking, just eating slowly, enjoying their hamburgers, hot dogs, and sandwiches. A certain rosy glow emanates from pink cheeks, permeating the entire room with the flushed contentment of sensual satisfaction.

"Hey, George," I whisper as we move up to the counter, "these people here look like they just survived a tidal wave. What the hell's goin' on? What kind of resort is this anyway?"

"The hamburgers are all right, but the egg salad sandwiches are outta sight," he answers with a stupid grin. He's relishing in his private knowledge of the place, and I'm getting a bit pissed off at this secrecy, feeling as though I'm about to undergo unprepared an initiatory ceremony of some secret sect.

"Look, damn it! Tell me what's goin' on! I'm beginning to feel like I entered another world! These people are like zombies and," I continue in a softer tone, "this guy on my right is lookin' at me with rape in his eyes or else I'm goin' batty!"

"Oh, here's Ed....Hi, Ed. How are the cesspools today?"

"Hello, George," he answers as friendly as can be, "haven't seen ya for a while. Resting up from the last time no doubt. We got the cold pool filled again, clogged pipes, and ya should've seen the muck. Y'know y'all should take showers before ya get in the baths. The pipes aren't what they used to be, and I'm too old for that kind of work. If I have to change the pipes, might have to up the admission fee. Now ya wouldn't want that, I know."

"Sure, Ed, I'll pass the word. Don't you worry. Hey, this here's my friend, Mike. First time up. You know, he tells me he finds it a bit strange around here."

"Hi, Ed," I say, trying to be friendly too.

"First time, huh? Well, my lad, you're in for a real treat. If you're here, there must be a good reason, for those who arrive at my portals come by what only can be called divine grace. You are one of the chosen, the elected, who by fate or supernatural law, have found the path to that straight gate by which one enters my Elysian Fields. Let me tell you also, that those who enter here leave behind their inhibitions and conventions, mores and morals, and, most important of all, their clothes. For here no modesty is necessary nor shame warranted. I have traveled over many lands in my day and have seen every sort of rite, ritual, custom and ceremony, and believe me, my boy, everything is right in its own place. So here do not be shocked by what your brothers and sisters out there would call perversions or unnatural acts, for here, in this spot, I have fulfilled my dream: a little corner in this green valley where one and all are welcome to frolic, romp and play in the hills and streams as wild nymphs and satyrs, to languish in the clear pools, bathe as did the Romans in ancient days, one and all, men and women, boys and girls, in natural harmony, leaving their bodily impulsions to take their course as God intended. So go enjoy yourself, my boy. For just a dollar upkeep you will have a little taste of paradise. Stay as long as you like, and do not fail to reap of the fruits proffered to you here in this, my garden of delights."

As he was spieling this out, I couldn't help but notice his face: not a wrinkle! Sixty years old, no doubt, and he was like a child. He had a certain appealing innocence, as though he had stopped growing, learning, at the age of ten.

"I'm beginning to get the drift of things, Ed," I respond, "but tell me, can just anyone come in here?"

"Well, at first I made no restrictions, but, you see, certain people simply don't know how to enjoy themselves, can't function without their clothes or uniforms, who sit and stare like stunned deer, making it uncomfortable for the rest. So contrary to my firm beliefs, my instincts even, I was forced to make a rule: no police or judges. But eat up and go enjoy yourself, talk is useless, though it seems I can't keep myself from extolling the benefits of my terrestrial paradise...."

"Funny old guy," I say to George as Ed walks over to a group coming up to the bar.

"Yeah," he answers with a smile, "I must have heard that spiel a hundred times already. Everybody calls him Crazy Ed."

"Perhaps not so crazy as all that, but you're right about these egg salad sandwiches. They're delicious!"

We pay our dollar entrance fee to paradise, go back to the car, take off our clothes, and walk briskly towards the bathhouse. I feel good being naked outside like this, really free, like a revolutionary. When we get next to the building George just says, "See ya later," and leaves me to discover what it's all about. For a while I just walk around outside, looking at whatever catches my eye. I even go into the forest a little way pretending, since I'm naked, that I belong to a primitive tribe, but I'm afraid of getting lost so I turn around and come back across a rickety wooden bridge spanning the stream, over to the mud baths and natural warm pools on the other side. I begin to feel a strange joy seeing all these naked people lounging around on the ground or playing in the stream. I begin to understand the warm sun, the river, the hills, and the trees. I become aware of the wind blowing lightly down the valley, mussing my hair. I feel happy and gay like a kid at the beach, just want to talk to someone, nothing serious, just blabber and play, so I go back to the bath house to see who's there.

It's an old stone crumbly building like a ruin of an ancient Roman bath. Inside, as I enter, it's dim and hard to see, though a greenish plastic roof lets through enough light to produce a chartreuse glow as if the steam was made up of phosphorescent vapors. Spears of sunlight coming through holes in the roof lace the rooms with bars that blind as I pass through them. Walking carefully on the slippery stones, my eyes adjusting, I soon discover the layout. There are three pools, all about ten by fifteen feet with water about six feet deep. Three pools: cold, warm, and hot, with little dressing cubicles surrounding them where you can leave your towel. There are showers in the middle and also a couple of small steaming sulphury saunas at the far end.

Being rather hot from the beating sun, my body takes me to the cold-water pool. There are seven or eight people hanging on the sides—young and old, men and women. They all look dead hanging there naked doing nothing in the glowing steam. I think it would be out of place to do laps, so I latch on to the side and say, "Hi, What's happening?" to no one in particular. No response, so I continue: "Is there some method to using these pools?" This brings a snicker from the girl next to me. I can hardly make her out what with the shadows and steam, but I don't like the way she laughed. "So, tell me what you do here then," I ask in an irritated tone. A guy across from me hands me a joint I haven't noticed before saying, "Here, don't do anything. Just smoke this and hang loose, man." I take a couple of drags, really deep ones, and pass it on. By the time it has gone around the pool two or three times, the water, the steam, and the green shadows are taking on fantastic shapes and I am hanging so loose that I lose my grip and sink down into the pool over my head. Even in the state I'm in, I can't help noticing as I'm going under that the water isn't the cleanest to be found. I thought the water was green from the reflection, but it's rather from the layer of scum that covers the surface and which leaves a coating of slime on the body. When I come back up somebody grabs my arms and someone else my legs.

They stretch me out in the water and begin massaging me all over, rubbing and squeezing.

"Don't worry," comes from a husky woman's voice reassuringly, "we're all friends here, so relax. We love you.

'Love me?' how nice, I think, as though mentally retarded, 'how nice.' So I close my eyes and keep thinking how pleasant it is to float in the cool water supported and caressed by people who love me. In the midst of the pleasure, panicky thoughts bubble up of demons; demons preparing me, putting me off guard, before pulling me down, holding me under as a sacrifice in some devilish ritual. The paranoia passes, however, and I continue to lay there thinking only of the sensual enjoyment I am experiencing.

Finally, after what seems a long while, when each of my limbs belongs to someone else, they let me go and another takes my place: a girl of about twenty with a roundish body. We all just knead her like dough, until after a while it's just flesh and more flesh, like making bread. This goes on through a couple more people, an older man and a young boy, and then I don't know how or why, but people start pairing off. In one corner, as I drift back to the side, I see the older man's head between another fellow's legs. A middle-aged lady, probably the one who spoke to me about love, seems to smile at me with gleaming pearly teeth. She glides over to me and huskily asks how I liked the massage. I don't say anything as she presses against me. I don't know what to do. I feel funny, her being so much older, like she's my mother or something. But the drug is sending me to places I've never been before, so I grab her, take her to me. I don't care. I don't care at all anymore, and it's wonderful as she wraps her legs around my back in the water while I slip it into her. As I agitate back and forth, funny noises come out of her mouth, little squeaks like a baby sparrow. When it's over she smiles with her pearly teeth, tells me she loves me, and goes on to the next fellow. My mind in a green fog, I go to see what is happening in the warm-water pool.

Here the mood is completely different. Maybe because there is more light in the room, and then, too, there are a lot more people. While before there was the silence of gliding bodies in dark water, here it's a veritable hubbub of agitated conversations. When I lower myself into the tepid water and find a place on the side, I begin to make out some of the topics being discussed. Most of it has to do with some sort of self-improvement of one type or another. I just listen for a while, enjoying the warm water, catching snaps of conversation out of the ripples of words that rise and fall and cut each other off....

> *"...controlling alpha waves through biofeedback...prefer shiatsu over Swedish massage...necessity of balancing the life energy through polarity manipulations...using the gestalt approach of Tibetan Buddhism, Vipassana or Hindu mantra meditation...vegetarian diet combined with juice fasting...in the morning Tai Chi and jogging...experience joy of the inner self..."*

Just on my left, a stocky man of about forty-five with a well-trimmed greyish goatee is extolling the benefits of "hyperconscious meditation" as a means of relaxing the body. As I hear it, he is getting quite upset at the thin young fellow in his twenties with the metal-rimmed glasses and thick mustache who simply will not understand the older man's viewpoint. For him, relaxation of the body should begin with the body and is a confirmed follower of a certain form, as he says, of "Reichian-gestalt bodywork similar in some of its theoretical aspects to Rolfing and connective tissue manipulation." He also is getting a bit hot under the collar—so to speak, that is, since like everyone else, he is naked, too. I can't help getting itchy listening to them. It's just my type of conversation. Not that I care who is right if anybody. I just love to talk about ideas, so I chime in with my two cents worth....

"If you don't mind my breaking in, I couldn't help overhearing your conversation and it seems to me that some sort of yoga technique incorporating both meditation and the *asanas* or physical postures might, in fact, be a synthesis between your two viewpoints."

"Well, that might be true in a sense," the older man rather condescendingly responds, "but, you see, hyperconscious meditation allows one to gain enlightenment through a half-hour a day of simple meditation. That's all that's necessary. Through the increased energy flow, the body itself is relaxed and you don't have to waste your time engaged in all these different postures, or, for that matter," turning to the young man with the metal-rimmed glasses, "go through some painful massage technique that turns your body inside out."

"Yes, of course, of course," the young man exclaims impatiently. "We're not really disagreeing. It's just a matter of approach. However, through bodywork, what may take you a year of meditation will take us only a month. The progress is simply much faster beginning with the body."

"But still," I can't help saying, "if one did both a meditative technique and some form of bodywork, wouldn't that be then twice as fast."

"Well, there might be something to that," the older man answers, "but, you know, one has only so much time for this sort of thing, there's always one's career, one has to live...."

At this point, I decide to glide over to the other side where I've been noticing a young man and woman in lively discussion. I've become curious as to what it is that seems of such obvious importance to them both. It has something to do with "consciousness expansion," as much as I can make it out hanging on to the side listening. The man, who has quite long blond hair, is an evident proponent of the use of LSD and other psychedelic drugs such as psilocybin and mescaline.

According to him, "Psychedelics, man, is the only way. When you're tripping, you're in other worlds. You understand what it's all about, like the universe. You are, you become what is, you follow? You become everything else, everything is you and you are everything. You know, the One, the All, Satori, Nirvana. You, your little insignificant miniscule, tiny good-for-nothing ego dissolves, disappears into the sacred realm of cosmic consciousness...."

"Yes," she interrupts, "but it's artificial, it's like take a pill and find paradise. It's not you, it's the pill. It's actually the worst thing, don't you see? Look, you think you're God already because you take some pills and have some funny experiences. You're all pride and bluster and you can hardly talk English anymore either. If you found Jesus like I have, then you would understand what I'm talking about."

"Find Jesus! Where did you find him? In the lost and found? Anyway, man, what's the diff? LSD or a dose of Jesus, as long as you get there, right?"

"The difference is love," she says with a great tone of finality. "Since I have found Jesus, I have learned to love everybody. I even love you even though I disagree with you. It is only when you feel love for all of God's creatures that you become one with the universe."

"You mean you love snakes and rats? Wow, I could never love rats, man, they give me the willies."

"Oh, don't be such a shitty nitwit! Of course, I don't really love rats, but I try to love rats at least. I'm not Jesus, you know."

"Not yet, anyway," he snickers popping a purple pill.

All of a sudden I find myself trying to harmonize their two positions saying, "You both actually may be right, you know, if my butting in is okay. Perhaps the use of drugs may be good as a tool, a means to get in touch with the unknown, the unconscious, or perhaps the superconscious; but having done so, having experienced another reality, it seems to me that then one should drop them and find a path, Christianity if you like, in order to realize this reality in oneself."

They both look at me, then at each other, and start to giggle. I don't know why. What did I say? He just grunts, "Yeah, man," while she goes off dog paddling around the pool.

It seems to me to be a good time to get out and try the next pool, the hot-water one. As I walk over thinking about what I said about consciousness, I bump into someone walking who calls me a clumsy oaf. I can't understand why I feel so uneasy, as though I've just told a lie. Everything I said seemed to have been right on the mark and well-presented, too.

Suddenly I'm standing at the edge of the pool. Looking down at the hot wisps of vapor rising, I realize all at once that I am totally alone. My first impulse is to return to the others, but I still feel uneasy and decide to stay here and think through some more what had been said. As I start to ease my feet into the water, I begin to understand why no one else is here: the water is incredibly hot, burning even. Yet something within wants me to immerse myself, a masochistic desire obliterating everything but the longing to burn takes over my mind. The flesh itself, however, wants nothing to do with it; but the desire overcomes the body's resistance, and slowly I begin to lower myself like a medieval victim into boiling oil. It is delicate work this, inch by inch, moving with every tiny let-up in the body's desire to spring from the stinging heat. Taut as a gazelle at the whiff of a lion, I take note of every sensation taking place in my body. My feet below the surface, under a ring of fire around the ankles, seem as though attacked by glowworms eating into the flesh. As I slowly work my way in, my legs feel as though bathed in magma, and then all at once I realize I've been holding my breath. I let it out in one huge gasp and, up to my waist now, begin to feel the heat penetrate into the muscles, tendons, cartilage, and bone. Now for some reason I don't feel "pain" anymore nor even "heat." Just a spreading, deepening sensation and all my joints unlock. The fear, too, that I hardly realize I had, begins to dissolve. The thoughts that were so important a few minutes ago now seem ridiculous, infantile, the drivel of a neurotic. Worries, judgments, all absurd now. All I am is pulsating sensation. My body throbs with each heartbeat. I'm the color of lobster. If the water started to boil, it would make no difference; I would just feel myself cook. I am up to my neck now and the sweat is pouring out of my face. I feel afraid. I get out and practically collapse like a rubber duck. I slither over to the showers and turn on the cold tap. The spray hits me like a hundred thousand darts of ice. In riveting pain my whole body contracts in one huge gasp. My lungs are sucked up into my mouth. Intense sensation, coursing energy....

I stride outside and am bedazzled by the sun, the hills, the sky. It's late afternoon, yet it is still hot. The heat feels good on my body, purifying. I take the narrow steps under the bridge, halfway down diving off into the stream, heedless of the danger of rocks. With hard, steady strokes I swim up the river against the current until I come to a large natural pool. There are people in it swimming or sunning themselves seal-like on the stones. I'm so full of energy that I dive to the bottom looking for treasure. Popping up like a dolphin, I spy George down by the waterfall. He's with a girl "George, George," I scream. He waves to me, and I dive back down, popping up again like a rubber ball, "George, George!" I go on like this for a while as though mentally deficient. Then just standing there in the waters without thinking, everything I see is shimmering with an iridescent brightness and clarity: the water like diamonds, the rocks like mosques. I feel so good I want to cry. The last thing I want is to talk. So I find a big fat boulder and lay spread-eagled on my back facing the sun. Some bizarre fellow comes up, puts his hand on my leg and starts talking about his sex drive. I kick him in the face. I begin to scrape my back up and down on the rock. Marvelous! I begin to bleed. The last thing remembered before drifting off into sleep is the hot sun penetrating, liberating....

When I wake up, it's already dark. It's strange to be nude in the dark outside....Yet it's warm and clear, and I wade back in the moonlight down the river to the bridge. At the top of the stairs I run into George with Mrs. Pearly Teeth on one arm and somebody he introduces as Louise on the other. Of course, they're all naked.

"Well, how do you like the Geysers?" George asks me, grinning like a cat.

"Splendid," I say, "What's next on the agenda?" and without waiting for an answer I put my arm around Louise cupping her breast. I pull her away from George and slide my hand down over her abdomen. Her body quivers like a lioness in heat as she responds cat-like to my touch, purring and arching her haunches up against my thighs. Mrs. Pearly Teeth asks if we would like to spend the night together in their campsite under the stars. No need to say anything. We just start walking across the bridge, Louise and I with arms around each other's waist, my hand resting lightly on her hip.

On the other side are the natural mineral pools, shallow depressions filled with water bubbling up warm from underground. In the middle of the largest one a couple is making love under a full moon, a shimmering bright disk casting silvery shadows over the water and rocks. We stop and stand around them to watch, and I become one huge cyclopean eye. I notice a mole on the man's left buttock and a blue clip in the woman's hair. They begin to look like fish floundering in a puddle after the tide's gone out, the water splashing out with each gyration.

As their rhythm increases, along with my own excitement, I begin to think, 'My God! Here I am, doing just what I've always fantasized about, a real orgy! So forbidden! So exciting! And yet, after they reach orgasm, and even in my almost feverish anticipation, as we walk through the brush into a clearing strewn with sleeping bags, I can't help feeling a certain uneasiness. I can't ascribe it to simple guilt from a moralistic upbringing. That has been burned out long ago. I don't know what it is, only that is the sort of feeling one has on taking a trip, halfway there, the horrible feeling that one has left something very important back home, and, for the life of one, can't think of what it might be, and that even if remembered, one has already gone much too far to turn back.

APPLE STRUDEL DANDY

A few weeks after our trip to the Geysers, sitting in our flat one evening smoking dope and listening to the Doors, George says to me, "Caroline is having a party Saturday night. It's going to be great. You've gotta go, it'll do you good."

I take George's advice, though I have to go alone: the Dead are doing the Fillmore and he managed to wangle a couple of tickets and one of his students to go with him. The party's taking place in some dingy club rented for the occasion in the flatlands of Berkeley. So long has it been that I've been to a party, I become at once excited and enthused, so enthused in fact that immediately upon entering the dim lit place I down three or four quick beers to calm my jitters, then ask the nearest available female to dance, which we proceed to do for the next three hours straight without a let-up. I can't stop even if I want to. The more I dance, the more energy I have. The faster the music, the better I like it. Like a man with a demon, my body has taken on a life of its own. I've become a *dybbuk* and I can't keep up with it. After a while I don't even try. I just jump and turn wriggle and squirm. I do splits like a Cossack. I kick like a mule. I crawl on my belly like a reptile. I begin foaming at the mouth, eyes spinning, shaking like a Haouka possessed. Leaping like a gazelle, I lose touch with my partner. Don't even speak one word to her the whole time. Isn't necessary, her being glassy-eyed herself. Finally we close the place. Only one thing left to do: go to bed. On the way out I almost blow it: I begin to talk, imagining it's the right thing to do. I find out she works in the neighborhood slave market, or as she calls it, "The Department of Human Resources."

"Didn't it used to be called the Department of Employment?" I ask her as we sail out the door.

"Yes," she laughs, "does that interest you?"

She has dark eyes and hair and a sensual mouth, things I hadn't even noticed up to now. Her smile is like an invitation.

"You know why they changed the name, don't you?" I ask, ignoring her question.

"No, I don't," she responds quizzically, "it must sound more efficient or something. Who cares anyway?"

"Well, it's really to hide the fact that there are thousands and thousands of poor slobs walking the streets without a job. Department of Employment implies that people need work, while the present euphemism suggests that the jobs are there, that it's the people, the resources that have to be found, like oil or gypsum."

Very proud I am of my little analysis, but her blank stare tells me she is more interested in something else, so I ask her if going to her place is okay. She smiles and says sure. I find out on the way over that she is expecting her boyfriend up from L.A. tomorrow to live with her. I suppose she wants one last debauch before turning herself into the faithful mate. We spend the night is some incredibly wild bed bouncing, which eventually leads to her getting me a job at Izzy's, a small Jewish bakery in Oakland. At the time, I thought the fates were with me, but if I only knew what I was getting into I would have strangled her that night in bed.

The job, being so far away, means I have to get up at 5:30 a.m., for it's no easy task getting to work without a car. Like the rest of the automatons, I catch the six o'clock trolley to the bus terminal, take the cross-bay bus to Oakland, then walk a good half-hour before reaching the shop, where my Lord and Master is waiting apron in hand, orders spilling out of his mouth like diarrhea before I can even kiss his hand.

"Weigh da shortenin'," he usually starts out, immediately followed in quick succession by "open da cherry cans, oil da dough, scrape da trays, grease da bread pans, measure da sugah, egg-wash da bread, sprinkle da sesame seeds, box da macaroons, crack da eggs, fill da proof-box, empty da oven, sweep da floors, wash da pots," and so on and so forth.

In between his orders to me, he spends his energy berating his wife Lilian who tends the shop up front selling the goodies we so carefully put together ("Not ready yet? What's da mattah wit' ya? Dat ordah fer Nathan's Deli shoulda been ready at ten! Ya tink I work like dis so's ya can fool around! Ya dumbbell!") Now and then she has enough of it and walks out. Though Izzy doesn't care. I don't know what happens at night, but she's always back bright and early the next day. And when by my look he sees that I think he's a real bastard for the way he treats her, now and then, in a fit of nostalgia, with tears streaming down his cheeks, he recounts to me his Jewish credentials, how he was captured by the English on the way to Palestine and thrown in a camp to rot.

I have to hand it to him, though; I've never seen anyone work so hard, 8:00 to 6:00 without a let-up. Sometimes he even screams at the mixer because it doesn't turn fast enough. I learn only later that he works like a maniac because he wants a three-day week-end in Reno with his mistress. This is explained to me by Helen who sometimes comes in to help in the afternoons. If it wasn't for Helen to talk to, I don't know what I would do. Her husband is a truck driver, and she too has worked all her life. When we're packing cookies together we have a chance now and then to exchange a few words, and she tells me of her work experiences in factories and sweat shops.

After the first couple of weeks, when the novelty has worn off and the shock of discovering myself as nothing more than a coolie has sunk in, a certain routine nevertheless establishes itself. Once a week, on Mondays, we make Izzy's specialty, his cheese, apple and cherry strudel for which he has no small reputation in Bay Area bakery circles. Making strudel is like a weekly religious rite for Izzy, I suppose because on the Sabbath he's always in the casinos of Reno rather than in temple and keeping kosher. It takes three of us an entire day to make enough strudel for the week, and for the occasion we always sanctify ourselves with a clean white apron. The ritual begins with Izzy anointing the carefully prepared dough with a thick coat of oil, which he places like a sacred relic on the three cloth-covered altar tables. Meanwhile, I measure against the weights three pounds of breadcrumbs on the bronze-plated scale. The next step is the real art of the ceremony, and a real art it is too, for Izzy has to stretch the dough bit by bit, corner by corner, not too slow, not too fast, so that without ripping, the dough overlaps the entire table like a precornered sheet of a nuptial bed.

"Yas, dat takes me years to know," he told me the first day we tried it together. "Da mixture iss very important. Da flour, da salt, da egg, da amount iss very important for to get da right consistency. An' da technique, fer yous it looks easy; if yous tried a 'unnerd times yous could not do it, a tousand maybe, if yous has talent. I learn it from da uncle in da olt country. Ain't no school teach yous dat."

The next step in the ceremony is the Sprinkling of the Breadcrumbs. This, too, though not an art, requires a certain technique into which I was initiated on my first Monday, for it is very important that the crumbs are spread evenly over the dough—absolutely no lumps or piles! Helen, of course, had long ago mastered the operation and has been given the task of teaching me this minor skill of the baker's art. After a couple of false starts Izzy shouts, "No, no! Yous iss not a woodsman. Dat iss not sawdust. Yous iss Tinkerbell an' dat is fairy dust. Yous see?" At times Izzy can be a real charmer, it's true.

I half-expect the dough to miraculously change into strudel, but Izzy picks up a funnel-shaped sack and squeezes out like toothpaste a thick roll of apple filling along one edge of the dough-covered table. It's a treat just to watch him, how he wrings and mangles the sack like a penitent, the filling oozing out, a worm that never dies. Now I run around the tables pulling off the dough hanging over the edges. "Like dey duz when dey circumcise da baby child," Izzy advises me. Then Helen comes up and rolls the filling in the dough, first one table then the next. Following her, Izzy sacrifices with neat strokes of his knife the long snake-like rolls which he then slips into well-greased pans. Another anointing of oil and into the oven. As each table is cleared, I have to respread the ceremonial cloth, consecrate it with flour and then the whole ritual begins again—and again, and again, and again the whole day long. After a couple of Mondays, we move along like well-oiled machinery, and when we have finished, when I have scraped and swept the floors, when I have washed the pans and scoured the pots, I am steadily rewarded like a faithful dog with a good size box of this succulent savory pastry.

I can always be sure that George will be waiting for me when I come home on these days, for he has taken a fantastic liking to the stuff. He has never tasted anything remotely like it on the plains of Indiana and he has quickly become addicted. He always has two finely rolled joints lying next to him on the arm of the overstuffed chair as I enter, and before biting in, we get thoroughly and marvelously stoned. Then, like little children with homemade sugar cookies, we munch in ecstasy Izzy's sacred strudel.

I have a hand in making all sorts of other delectable delicacies, every kind of savory pastry, cookie, pie, and sweet creamy cake. Like every job, it has its payola, and I am allowed to eat as much as I want while I work: lemon napoleons, rich custard eclairs, or whatever else is in reach. At the end of the week, I'm given a big pink box of the pastries of my choice. Needless to say, my waistline has noticeably enlarged. Making the Danish cheese is my favorite task, however; not only because I am left to myself for an hour or so instead of running around like a slave at the whim of the bagel king, but also because it produces a strange sensual satisfaction. After Izzy has laid out the dough on a big wooden table and cut it up into squares, it is then my job to oil it well, add a gob of cheese in the center, and then, after carefully folding up the corners like laundry in a sheet, to place a finger in the center, on the collected corners, and push through the squishy cheese to the table leaving a little hole. Now every time I do this, that is, push my finger down through the cheesy dough, a little shiver tingles over my entire body. When I first started this operation, I couldn't understand what was producing this bizarre sensation, except that I had the strange feeling of having done this sometime before. Enough be said that I am always left with a tremendous aching erection—which gets to be quite embarrassing, what with Helen and Lilian walking back and forth all the time.

I have innumerable other little tasks, such as putting strawberries in tarts, dipping cookies in chocolate, or just mixing the sugar, lemon juice and preservatives which I cook with the apples in the big copper kettle. It isn't all fudge and butterscotch work, however. An afternoon making breadcrumbs is enough to leave any man sore. Now breadcrumbs are not what one sweeps up from the floor. Crumbs are made, and it's a hell of a job! First, I have to scrape clean about fifteen shallow pans, removing the encrusted, burnt-in remains of yesterday's apple turnovers or Black Forest cherry cake. After oiling the pans, I plop the previously prepared dough in the middle of each pan, and this dough is in no way like the soft strudel dough but has more the consistency of quick-hardening plaster, especially if I use, as I once did, Sweetex instead of Primex shortening (a fact which Izzy never fails to remind me of if I dare to offer an idea to ameliorate some mind-deadening procedure). Now I have to knead, beat, shove this lump of cement until it covers the entire pan, a feat worthy of a wrestler's masseur. With every pounding of my fist, every grunt of effort, I can't help but ask myself what for God's sake I'm doing here. Once I just couldn't take Izzy telling me what to do. I started screaming and yelling, jumping up and down, "Leave me alone, damn it!" I shouted, "You don't have to tell me how to beat the fuckin' dough!" I quickly took advantage of his astonishment to demand ten-minute breaks in the morning and afternoon. In any case, after all the pans have been spread with dough, I put them in the oven until they're cooked brown, take them out and slam the bread out of the pans onto the table, cut them up into little pieces with a huge slicing knife, and dump as much as possible into the mixer, grinding them up into the crumbs that I later sprinkle over this or that pastry, cake, or pie.

A couple of times a week I'm paroled from the ovens in order to make deliveries. Sometimes it's pastries and strudel to a Jewish deli in San Francisco or perhaps a Middle Eastern restaurant in San Mateo. Other times it's a bar mitzvah cake, a yard square, replete with candy torahs and Israeli flags, for a synagogue hidden up in the Santa Cruz Mountains. Or, in

Oakland itself, I'll bring to a Jewish old-age home an order of thirty loaves of twisted *challah*, that egg-rich, sesame-sprinkled bread that, if compared to the mixture of chemicals and air which Americans are used to, could only be called some kind of rich yellow cake. Izzy is a talker, a real businessman, for every place I deliver seems to believe that what I bring is Izzy's only specialty. At Jacob's in the City, for example, it's *binen stitch*, layers of thin flaky crust, thick lemon custard, and orange sponge cake all topped with nuts and caramel cream; or at the Coffee Clatch it's either the eclairs or the cream rollers, those spiraled rolled-up crusts filled with whipped cream and tipped with a thick coat of chocolate, very popular with the older ladies. Once every two weeks I replenish Harry's Deli in Berkeley with different kinds of cookies: chocolate florentines, jelly crescents, sugar rings, meringue kisses and vanilla *kiepfel*. Alexander's in Castro Valley, on the other hand, doesn't order anything but lemon napoleons, rum balls, and the thick nougat slices that nobody can resist for long.

I always look forward to Wednesdays, for it's then that I deliver the challah and bagels to the Jewish old-age home only a few blocks away. It seems so incongruous as I walk in, the kitchen full of blacks cooking blintzes and matzah ball soup for the old people left to die. After a while I get to know some of the cooks and we make jokes about kosher chitlins. Sometimes if they're taking a break, if no one is there, I'll wait in the kitchen and just smell the rich Jewish food cooking and steaming, the Jewishness exuding even from the walls, while I listen to the warbling strains of cracked voices sifting through the corridors:

> *Hava Nagila, hava nagila*
> *Hava nagila, v'nism'cha cha*
> *Hava n'ran'na, hava n'ran'na*
> *Hava n'ran'na, v'nism'cha cha....*

91

Just sitting here, trance-like, transformed by the music, the odors, the old country accents, opening channels to memories long forgotten of happier days: the huge Passover table, the seder, opens up in my mind as out of a mist, with the uncles, the aunts, the innumerable cousins, sitting there each in our place. "Why is this night different from all other nights?" I ask to begin the ritual. To which my father would intone the response reading from the *Haggadah*. Step by step the ritual continued, the plate of bitter herbs, of unleavened bread, the *haroses* and all the rest, which my mother had so carefully prepared during the day. Each dish explained in terms of Jewish history, a people confirming their identity after being dispersed for 2,000 years. This strange Hebrew language which to my young mind seemed so mysterious and the hiding of the matzah which the children had to find to gain their reward. How we loved that in our innocence. And then, too, the mystery of opening the door for Elijah. Open a door for someone who never came? Why? Why? I only had questions then, and in my naiveté and childish hope, I would often take furtive glances at the doorway, half-expecting an old man in white robes to miraculously appear take his place at our table. Innocence and mystery, openness and wonder, this childhood so far away and long ago. What snapped here between these generations that let in the insanity, the drunkenness, the drugs, the dizzying search for a place to lay one's head?

Lost in these images and thoughts, I don't even notice Mr. Greenbaum until he shakes me by the shoulder, waking me from my reverie, anxious as he is to pay and settle the bill, a nervous crotchety old bastard with his little black book marking down the day's accounts as carefully as a soldier marks his calendar.

What bothers me most about the job, however, is that I feel I'm wasting my time. I'm only here to make money, and that's no reason to do anything I tell myself. But what other reason can I give for my slavish condition? Not that I have any idea of what I would do with my time if I wasn't working, but somehow I feel that this work is beneath me. A belief in my own importance has unknowingly been instilled, that certain work is below me, that my place is to contemplate, to think, to ponder. What strange psychological quirk has taken hold of me? What demonic force keeps saying: "You are guilty! You are guilty!" Every situation, job, group, or person I become involved with leads inexorably to one desire: flee! Escape from a world that has become a cage. People are but vampires wanting only to suck my individuality, organizations snares whose sole purpose is to entrap me into conformity. I cannot resist, preserve myself, keep my own identity in face of the world. I ebb and flow with everything around me. I do only what is expected of me. The whole world has become my enemy and I am the king of my own arid realm.

For reasons I have yet to fathom, I begin to see this strange uncontrollable creature, this other self, this *Doppelganger*, and I think I am going mad. In truth, I think I have seen myself before the time. Yet, I have to work like everyone else and what do I care what I do in a world in which I don't belong. All work is ridiculous to me, a way to eat and pay the rent. It's on the same level as stealing and borrowing, below even, since working takes up much more time. But day after day of pummeling and kneading the dough brings the reality of my situation closer and closer to the truth until I can't think further than the bottom of the filthy pots I am scouring. This is what I am doing! This is what I am! Five years of university and here I am a washerwoman, a floor scraper, a failure of the lowest sort. Me, with my intellectual pretensions, pretending to understand the world, the universe, the great questions of the age and now face to face with the beast, unable to figure out how to live my own life! My God, aren't I one of the chosen people? How is it that I ended up on the bottom, no more than a servant, a serf? Any rationalization will do; led astray by women no doubt, and in our sick materialistic society to be a success, doesn't that mean to sell your soul? In our age isn't everything reversed; isn't this the Outer Darkness where to succeed is to fail and failure the door to salvation? Doesn't it say that it is easier for a camel to go through the eye of a needle than for a rich man to enter the Kingdom of God? Doesn't it? Doesn't it say that the first shall be last, and the last shall be first? Doesn't it say that? Isn't this the *Kali-Yuga*, the Dark Age, where everything is upside down and inside out?

How many books have I combed looking for a word of comfort, a phrase of support, a sentence of understanding? I can't really discuss my problems with George, for we're both so intent on justifying our lives to ourselves and others that neither of us will give an inch on anything. So, like a gopher I dig into my library intent on unearthing the golden Word that will give meaning to my confused and miserable life. I never go anywhere without a book, or two or three. And then I begin to take notes, voluminous notes, with exact quotes and page numbers, a scholarly habit from the university. I practically copy word for word all the works of Nietzsche and Kierkegaard, not to mention Montaigne, Pascal, Unamuno and Herzen. I even began to read the Old Testament to find some solace, some relief from the worm:

> *...who led thee through that great and terrible wilderness wherein were fiery serpents, and scorpions, and drought, where there was no water; who brought thee forth water out of the rock of flint;*

> *Who fed thee in the wilderness with manna, which thy fathers knew not, that he might humble thee, and*

that he might prove thee, to do thee good at thy latter end....

I sift and scour book after book, taking a phrase here, an aphorism there, trying in any way possible to rationalize my incompetence. When I come across this sentence of Kierkegaard, for example, one particularly desperate day, it sets me up for a week:

> *But working for a living cannot be the meaning of life, since it would be a contradiction to say that the perpetual production of the conditions for subsistence is an answer to the question about its significance....*

In reading a book, certain passages jump out of the page and I become transfixed, stuck like a broken record, reading them to myself over and over. Yes! I say, Yes! Of course, that's right, that's right! And it becomes desperately important to write them down, to keep a record of them. This sentence of Henry Miller, for example:

> *On the surface, where the historical battles rage, where everything is interpreted in terms of money and power, there may be crowding, but life only begins when one drops below the surface, when one gives up the struggle, sinks and disappears from sight.*

Books, books, books! It's come to the point where books have become life and life but a dream. One day, when I am in the bus on the way to work, in the middle of the bridge and seriously thinking of jumping out and leaping into the icy depths below, on this day I open up a book I've stolen from the library and that is now laying in my lap: *The Letters of Vincent Van Gogh.* I open the book haphazardly and begin to read, and what I find myself reading is a paragraph that burns into my cortex like a battery of laser beams. So desperate am I for an answer, so much in need of a goal, that the whole world dissolves around me, all and everything becomes as a black blur—the bus, the people, the bridge, the water, the city, and the hills in the distance—stricken from my perception, my consciousness, my world. The sky itself is no more; it is just me and the Word, a spark glowing in the dark:

> *What am I in most people's eyes? A nonentity, or an eccentric and disagreeable man—somebody who has no position in society and never will have, in short, the lowest of the low. Very well, even if this were true then I should want my work to show what is in the heart of such an eccentric, of such a nobody.*

I suppose there are many who could pass that off as a well-turned phrase, but for me it is like a blind man seeing for the first time, or a monk focusing on the illuminated manuscript held reverently before his eyes. What I now understand is that what counts in this world is for a man to be himself. Yes, 'very well...' I will do my work, and if I cannot please you, if I cannot do what you want of me, I am sorry, it cannot be helped. For what I am and what I could be has nothing to do with the status, role or position I happen to have *by chance* in the society I was born into—*by chance!* What counts is my work as it corresponds to my nature. If I become wealthy by my work, if I become famous by what I do, that is by chance and chance only; but if I realize myself through my work, this is a matter of commitment, a willing of the self to create a Self, a destroying and a building up, an infinite longing for something more, much more, than a check from social security and a gold watch after thirty years. Yes, 'very well...' to accept a loss of station in the hope of creating something better, to nurture a hope based only on an inkling of an idea of what could be. Well, 'then I should want my work to show what is in the heart...' How it all seems so clear! How could I have been so blind! When I get off the bus I am so happy to get to work that I run all the way and, being early, pick up all the papers lying around the garbage cans. On this day the thought has entered that perhaps one day I, too, will in some way be a creator.

LETTERS FROM THE DESERT

After one particular god-awful day, on the bus going home, trying to understand what led me to this pitiful job at the bakery, my thoughts take me back to the first work I managed to find after leaving the university....

Trudging up a hill, a heavy sack of letters, junk mail and magazines on my back. The heat is intense and the sweat is pouring out. One foot after another, right-left, right-left. What does old man Ballin, my bull-faced supervisor, care if I sprained my ankle yesterday. What does he care if it's hot enough to fry an egg on the sidewalk. "No lame excuses, Allswang, get out and deliver the mail." The life-blood of the country I am, hand-delivering all the letters and bills, each invoice and payment. Climb fifty stairs, no mailbox to be found. It's on the side of the house, next to a dog the size of a rhino. I chance it, can of mace at the ready. Get away with torn trousers, dog eats the letter. Horseshoe it down the street, pick up the relay. Seems everyone reads magazines on the block and thick ones to boot. Up another hill, the sack heavier and heavier. A dog barks as I finger the mail in the street. Drop the letters, a car runs them over. Bend down to pick 'em up, magazines fall out of the sack. Re-sort the mail. Up the hill again, right-left, right-left. A misrouted letter, go back ten houses, don't pass 'go', don't collect nothin'—except a sore back. A dog barks, drop the letters again. Back up the hill, the day hotter and hotter, the sack heavier and heavier....

Every day it went like that, every day for a solid year. The only job I could get after I got out of the university. Not a teaching job to be had in the whole fifty states. I, the merchant's son, who was going to be a great thinker, an intellectual giant, a sequoia of the mind towering over the scraggly shrubs of modern thought, was now delivering mail for the United States Post Office, wearing the grey uniform, carrying the leather sack.

"Case up Route 16, Allswang," Ballin would bellow as I walked in the station at six in the morning. "And when you get finished with that, help out Johnson on Route 22. And don't futz around out on the street. You've got twenty bundles of mark-ups waiting for you when you get back."

That's how it started out after punching in and casing up the mail. Two or three hours a morning it was, taking the mail from the big grey sack (don't forget the labels!) and putting all the letters in their little slots and all the flats in their big compartments. Letters and flats, letters and flats, discussing soap operas and jazz concerts with the black lady carriers.

Everything was going so smooth, everything was going so fine up to then. One step after another all laid out there by society so I could have a marvelous career in academia. Then I was sorting letters, delivering the mail, fighting off dogs. Everything was so ordered before that, a straight line to the American dream. It was a shock that turned my world upside down and inside out. I became a walking automaton. If you turned me to the left, I walked left. If you turned me to the right, I walked right. If you liked waffles with ketchup, I liked waffles with ketchup. If you talked with an accent, I talked with an accent, the same. It was a damn good thing I had this job; or I would've stayed in bed until they buried me in it. Had no reason to do a thing. Eat and sleep were the only things I could manage. All I asked of the world was that someone tell me what to do, and my supervisor was glad to oblige.

Everybody likes the mailman which was good for my morale. Rich or poor, black or white, almost everyone wanted to be on my good side. Maybe they felt I had a certain power over them, that I was going to tear up their stock dividends or welfare checks if they gave me any lip. I couldn't understand at first why everyone was so nice to me, but when I understood what it was about, the idea that I had any power over anyone naturally led me to take advantage of the situation. If someone didn't come to the door fast enough to sign for a registered letter, for example, I would keep their Playboy Magazine and take it home to read for a week, usually at meals. I don't know what they thought when they saw syrup and mustard stains on the centerfold. Or, if I felt someone wasn't paying me the proper respect, ignoring me, for example, in passing me on the street, I would take what looked like their most important letters and leave them at my apartment for a month or so. I had a whole suspense file that I checked every day to see which letters I should bring back into circulation. Sometimes a person would ask about a letter that didn't show up, as if *I* was responsible, so I would make a note of it, and when I got home put it off for delivery for another couple of weeks. Pretty soon I had a file on everyone on my route. It was all organized on how much respect I was shown: the more respect, the better the service. Some people, just nasty by nature, never received any mail. If I didn't just throw their letters in the gutter, I would simply scrawl "unknown" on them even before I left the station and stick them in the "return to sender" box.

After a while, as I got to know people on my route better, I would decide for them what reading material I thought they should be receiving. Mrs. Harris, a case in point, impressed me as a real dumb bunny, so I would leave her the science magazines that Professor Schmidt down the block subscribed to, hoping thus to improve her intellectual capacities. Sometimes I would leave all the unmarked manila envelopes that I had steamed open at home to check on their contents, which for the most part were sex manuals and porno books, on the doorstep of Mrs. Vedette, who was a real prude if there ever was one. Towards the end of my year at the post office it came to the point where I started writing letters to some of the people, anonymously of course. To beautiful young ladies I would write passionate love letters, not hesitating to throw in a few crude suggestions when it pleased me to do so. The day after I delivered the letter, I would make up some excuse to ring the bell and as I talked to them about an undeliverable parcel, I would get an exquisite enjoyment in knowing they had just read my latest sexual fantasies. To more intellectual types, depending on their interests, which I knew from the magazines they received, I would expatiate for pages on the most abstruse subjects: "The New Physics and Its Relation to Philosophy," for example, or "The Mind: Individual or Universal?" It was a good thing I left the job about this time, as some people were beginning to give me strange looks. Besides the complaints had started to come in thick and fast on my route because of all the delayed deliveries and old Ballin was about to open an investigation. Now that I look back on it, I could have gone up on a federal rap.

I wore my hair long at the time, almost down to my shoulders. It stuck out of my hat like I was a mad scientist or a shaman. In the snobby hills of Piedmont I was often looked at askance when they thought I wasn't looking—which they paid for dearly, of course. In the flatlands of Oakland, however, I was often accepted as the "hippy mailman," and now and then I was invited in for a joint as I did my rounds. There was this one house especially that was a sort of commune or crash pad. All I knew was that there were always fifteen to twenty people lounging around stoned no matter what time of day I came by. A fellow named Richard was the leader it seemed, at least he was the one who invited me in one day as the joints were being passed. I was glad for the opportunity to take a rest, so I went in. It was some really far out stuff they were passing, and pretty soon I was really spacey. After a while some freak started giggling. He kept going and couldn't stop. Somebody asked him what was so funny. He responded that it just cracked him up to see a mailman in uniform with long hair and stoned silly. Then somebody else looked at me and started laughing. Soon everyone was doubled over in hysterics over me, and I couldn't help but join in. Then they started going into my sack passing out the magazines. It was the first of the month so there were plenty for everyone. After a while I asked if anyone wanted seconds and passed out some more. Then the freak started tearing out the pages, making paper airplanes that he sailed around the room chuckling uncontrollably. Not to be outdone, I tore out even more pages and made Chinese lanterns, one for each. All of us were laughing crazily and I liked that and didn't want it to stop, so I started opening up some letters and reading them, which brought on even fits and convulsions. The love letters were the funniest, especially the desperate ones threatening suicide if the beloved wouldn't return or get married or just answer one of his or her tearful, pleading messages. As one of these missives went around the room an ash fell on it making a hole. This gave Richard the idea of burning it, which he then proceeded to do. Before we knew it, we were throwing into the chimney everything in the sack: letters, bills, checks, journals, newspapers, publicity, manuscripts, books. I figured people would be much better off without all these accouterments anyway; it would make their lives simpler, easier to handle. Then the freak had the great idea of roasting marshmallows as we watched it all burn; so we all sat around the chimney and did just that, chewing in satisfaction as the flames licked through the mound of paper....A day well spent I thought as I got up to leave, and, having nothing more to deliver, I went home and slept like a baby lamb.

The mailman, like the barman, is a confessor of sorts. Instead of old men, though, it's the old maids and widows. The passing of the mailman, being their most exciting event of the day, would be cause to silver their hair and brush their bridges. The moment I turned the corner they would start puttering around their rose bushes or walking the dog. When I came up they would latch on like bloodsuckers recounting their tales of woe. I knew the diseases of every spinster, the family tragedies of every widow. I stood there and listened to it all, pretending interest in their arthritis and gout, the ungratefulness of their sons and daughters. So desperate to talk they were, I hadn't the heart to tear myself away. I began to take it as part of my job: taking on their problems, offering a word of consolation, a small piece of advice. Nobody could understand it at the station when for Christmas I received armloads of cigarettes, chocolates, and not a few bills of higher denomination.

Of course, what I was hoping to meet was some frustrated housewife who wanted nothing more than to throw herself into the arms of the mailman the moment her husband left for the office. No matter how many piercing looks I gave as I asked them to sign a receipt or take in a parcel, I never seemed to get the high sign, that is, until about a month before I left the service. It was a rich neighborhood up in the hills, on the boundary between Oakland and Piedmont. I was given a new route to replace someone who had gone on vacation. I had been on it a week already, delivering the usual bills and letters, when one Monday I had a certified letter to be signed for. I had cased up early that day and was out on the street at eight sharp. I rang her bell not much later. It was a two-story Spanish style with a huge front lawn. When she came to the door, I almost fainted. She had this nightie on, practically sheer, and a bathrobe left open hiding nothing of the gorgeous roundness of her flesh. I didn't say anything. I just stared until she realized the effect she was having on me. Blushing slightly, she pulled her bathrobe closed, mumbling something about just getting up.

"That's all right," I said with a grin. "No harm done, none at all. If you would just sign for this letter, please."

Nothing happened for the next couple of days, and all I could do was rack my brains for an excuse to ring her bell. But it wasn't necessary. The next day as I was slipping letters in her slot, she opened the door, bathrobe closed, however.

"Oh, I'm glad I didn't miss you," she said. "Could you mail these letters for me, please? It'll save me a trip to the corner."

Caught by surprise, all I could answer was "Sure, of course." Then she smiled at me and shut the door. I just stood there a second like a moron, then started kicking myself up and down the block for not starting up a conversation. 'Save a trip to the corner'? The mailbox was only three houses away. Maybe she wanted to talk to me, I thought, and who knows where it might have led. 'Next time I'm going to have something ready to say even if she opens the door stark naked!'

I figured it was my turn to make a move, so a couple of days later I rang her bell.

"Yes?" she asked in the same bathrobe after opening the door.

With all the courage I could muster I said, "I know this is quite unusual, but I woke up late and didn't have time for coffee this morning. Do you think you could give me a cup?"

She didn't respond right away, and I could tell from the questioning smile on her face that she was weighing things in her mind. She knew damn well what I was asking and it had nothing to do with coffee. From the slight purse of her lips I could tell she wanted it, too, but now that the opportunity was right there in front of her, all the business of the husband, the kids and the happy home was racing through her mind.

After looking at me up and down and with a little sigh she said, "Okay, why not? Come on in. I just put the pot on."

She was at least fifteen years older than me, for sure. She might have been "just a housewife," as they say, but from the casual way she went about my being there, with her in her bathrobe early in the morning, I figured this probably wasn't the first time something like this had happened. In fact, as I sat down at the kitchen table I made a mental reminder to myself to compare notes with the milkman and the meter reader.

"Why don't you take off that stupid-looking cap," she says, "it hides all that beautiful blonde hair of yours."

"Okay," I respond in the spirit of the game, "if you'll take off that bathrobe that's hiding all your beautiful flesh. Ever since you came to the door the other day with it wide open, I haven't been able to think of anything else. I've become obsessed."

Obviously flattered, she turns away from the stove, looks me right in the eye, and undoes the belt of her robe. It falls away exposing the same flimsy nightie hiding nothing of what's underneath.

I'm about to explode, but somehow I think I ought to say a little something before attacking her like a brute beast.

"Aren't you afraid your husband may come home unexpectedly, or one of the kids if you have any?" I ask as if I cared about her welfare, my eyes glued to her body.

"No, don't worry about him. He's one of those nine to nine types. Then the beer and television. If he found us in bed together, I'd tell him we were discussing the size of the mailbox and he'd believe me, the jerk. I would've left him long ago if it wasn't for the kids. And don't worry about them. They'll be in school all day. Come on, you don't have to make conversation with me. I think we both know what we want."

With that, I get up from the table spilling the coffee and push her against the stove all the while trying to kiss her and fondle her ass. She lets out a scream as she touches the burner, pushing me back.

"Careful, that's hot," she says.

"Sorry. Look, why don't we go into the bedroom. It'll be much more comfortable."

She walks over to the bed dropping the robe and nightie as she goes. Lying back open and willing, she holds her arms out to me. I undress quickly and climb over her like a man lost in the desert struggling over a dune. As she wraps her arms and legs around me, I sink into her like into quicksand, between her large breasts and thighs, into oblivion, into peace....

By the time I got out of there an hour later, I was sure it would be a month or so before I'd be able to go at it again. I'd never seen a woman so hot. I felt like asking her how long it had been, but I didn't want her to think there was anything unusual about her desire, afraid she'd hold herself in. It went on like that, too, for a couple of weeks at least—until I was transferred back to my usual route. She just waited for me every morning after hubby and the kids had gone off—soon without the robe, then without the nightie.

Not ever caring to finish the route after that, I just kept stuffing what was left into the corner mailbox every day—which kept coming back in sacks the next morning. Pretty soon I had three times as much mail to deliver as anybody else, and before Ballin got wise I brought the sacks home and left them there, that is, until I took them to the dump one evening before turning in....

During the Christmas rush we had to do overtime, sorting packages at the downtown terminal. I felt like a factory hand from another century. Even if they tried, they couldn't have built a more depressing place. It was this huge rectangle of a building made out of corrugated iron and thick plastic held together by a few iron beams that you could hear rusting as you worked. There were so many tubes and pipes and thick wires slithering up the walls, across the ceiling, over the floors, the place looked like a snake den from the Middle Ages—not to mention the conveyor belts that rattled and clanked without a let-up from the moment you arrived until you wobbled out the door. Some of the more prudent among us tried to take out insurance against going deaf, but since we were there for only two weeks not a company would handle it.

The first day we arrived we were put at our stations. "Now this is what you do," the supervisor there said, "You pick up the packages coming along the conveyor belt and look at the zip code. Then you put it in one of the sacks next to you corresponding to that number. If a package doesn't match one of the sacks, put it in the orange one on the end for rerouting. When a sack gets filled, take it off, put it on the belt behind you, label a new sack and put it up where the old one was. You got it? Any questions?"

"You mean this is what we're supposed to do eight hours a day?" I couldn't help exclaiming.

"Yes, why?...Don't worry, you get a half hour for lunch and a ten-minute break in the afternoon."

He added the last part when he saw how dumbfounded I was.

"Why don't you just open the homes for the mentally retarded and bring them down here to do the job," I continued. "It'd save you a lot of money and make them feel useful at the same time, don't you think?"

I was already going batty after two days at this business, and I couldn't imagine in the least how people worked down here *all the time!* That is, until one day when I was told to help load a truck. I was throwing sacks from the dock into a semi-trailer when a long-hair on the pile asked me to take his place. When I got into the truck, I couldn't help noticing the sweet smell of some grass, and climbing up to the top, I saw on the other side a group of workers passing around a joint. They motioned me down and, of course, I took a hit and then another and another. It seemed as if everyone on the floor would come over from time to time, like a trail of ants, and stoke up. From the dock, the truck looked like it was packed solid, and the supervisors, always busy making sure the right packages went into the right sacks and the right sacks into the right trucks, they never suspected a thing, ignoramuses that they were.

After that, the days went by in a haze. It was the only way to get through a job like that. Everybody did it. I'm surprised anybody got any Christmas packages at all. Stoned as I was, sometimes I didn't even look at the zip codes, just throwing the packages from one sack to the next in order, or, on the contrary, throwing all the packages into one sack until it was filled. Once I got a package for the governor of the state—I sent it off to Barstow. Another time it was to the police chief—I put it in the foreign sack for Singapore. I must admit I didn't have the guts, but some of the workers would just back their cars up to the dock, opened the trunk and slipped in a few sacks of presents. During Christmas, the children of the postal workers must be the happiest kids around.

After that experience, I never complained again about being a letter carrier. I even began to feel that I had certain amount of status in the postal service. I started trying to do my job well, to see if I could finish the whole route before lunch and get a pat on the back from Ballin, who rewarded me with a couple hours of paperwork to do or by having me finish up a route of somebody new. I might have even ended up spending my life there if it wasn't for the strike....

"They've gone out in New York!" This was the word buzzing around the station as I came in one cold January morning. Back East the agitation had been building up for some time, which was understandable given the pitiful wages we received. Out here in laid-back California, the most to be heard was the usual grumbling about not being able to make ends meet, that it was a damn shame, in this rich country, to work like we do only to receive a handful of peanuts. The unions, as usual, were in cahoots with the government and wanted nothing to do with the strike. Seems it was a wildcat: despairing over the union's inaction, the rank and file in the Big Apple one fine day just laid down their sacks and said the hell with it to everybody. The reaction in the Oakland office was predictable: threats from the government about being fired, wise counsels from the union not to do anything hasty, old-timers telling us youngsters to let those in authority do the necessary. They made me sick, all of them! Those guys in New York were putting their jobs right on the line! The whole thing was illegal from start to finish and they didn't even have the union to back them up!

And if they won, I would benefit as much as they. How could I just go on working? That would be the real crime, at least that's how I thought about it.

The trouble was I didn't want to lose my job. How hard it would be to find another one, and there's nothing I hate more than looking for work if it isn't working itself. But maybe if I put out real hard for just a week or so, I can get old Ballin on my side, and if I take any action maybe he'll put in a good word for me with the higher-ups, tell them what a good worker I am, when the shit hits the fan. I even cut my hair and shined my shoes. I talked pleasantly with everyone on the route, which was a real effort, hoping someone would call in and compliment me to the supervisor, all the while attending meetings of radicals and other assorted leftists planning our own underground action to close down the whole Oakland post office.

Every time I tried to get the carriers in my station interested in the strike going on back East, nobody wanted to even hear about it. Leave it to the union, they'd say. When I responded that the union was against the strike and that it was necessary to work against the union, too, they started getting a bit teed off. Who was I, they told me, a rank newcomer to the service, to say what should and should not be. When it got back to the union rep in my station that I was "agitating" among the carriers, he called me over one day and in no uncertain terms let me know that he would get me fired if I continued. When I pointed out to him that I thought it a bit strange that he, a representative of the union, was threatening me with dismissal and not the government, he responded that I had obviously been reading too much Marx and that I had better get wise as to how things stood, at the same time rubbing his fist with the other hand. So, now it was threats! I was so disgusted with the hypocrisy of it all, I was ready to quit right then and there and look for a job as a dishwasher, but I thought better of it and before leaving, asked Ballin if he had some extra work he wanted done, dusting his desk, for example, or sweeping the floor, on my own time of course, I added, when he looked a bit surprised.

Finally, the day arrived. We threw up a picket line in front of the main terminal preventing the trucks from taking the mail to the district stations. A mere twenty of us working in shifts closed down the whole operation. Not a truck was driven over by a worker. We got huge headlines in the local paper: "Huge Oakland Postal Center Closed Down," it said. Nobody could understand what was happening. The unions and the government had gotten together and reached their own little *modus vivendi*, and they couldn't figure out who we were. But we didn't care if anybody knew who we were; we did what we set out to do—we closed it down!

The FBI came down and took our pictures, people we didn't even know would bring us coffee and donuts in the early morning cold, then sandwiches for lunch and roast chicken for dinner. I felt like a real union organizer, like Big Bill Haywood, until the chief of the whole Oakland Post Office came up and asked me my name, pen in hand. I was paralyzed with fright. What are they going to do to me? I thought. Maybe they'll throw me in jail for a hundred years, put me on a blacklist so I'll never work again, take away my passport, fire me for sure. I couldn't say a thing. I felt like sinking into the ground. Why did he have to come up to me anyway? Here I was, fighting for a just cause minding my own business, spending long hours on the line, depriving myself of sex and sleep, practically a workingman's hero, and he had to come and single me out. When he saw the scared and sheepish expression on my face, as if I'd just gotten found out, he spat on the ground in front of me and walked away. God, I felt awful.

Nothing was the same after that. I was even sort of glad when, the next day, the union and the government worked out a plan to bust the strike by having the management drive the trucks through the line.

Part of the agreement of the nation-wide settlement was no reprisals to any worker. While I wasn't fired, it was true, I started gettin transferred all over the city, every day a different route—and Ballin didn't even lift a finger for me. They knew what they were doing for sure. I was going raving mad trying to find where people hid their mailboxes. It takes three or four runs before getting to know a route, and I had to start fresh every day. It took me twice as long as usual and I had to really push it just to get back on time. I saw the writing on the wall and figured it just wasn't worth the struggle, so one day I left hanging for good the big leather sack

BERZERKELEY

On my days off from work, I sometimes go to Berkeley, maybe to buy a book at Moe's on Telegraph Avenue, or more often than not, just to walk around bathing in the insanity. Berkeley, a little enough town of 150,000 souls and its huge university, the matrix of social and political, millinery and millennial movements in the United States, is a hodgepodge of every sort, of individualism, socialism, religion, party, sect, faction order, splinter group and off-shoot. People from Europe, I notice, always take New York as the center of innovation, California being identified only with "crazy hippies." I try to explain to them that New York is rather the refinery, the distillery, of the raw, steaming sump of Berkeley ooze, that from the miasma of revolutionaries and saints, agitators and agents provocateurs, of shop lifters and pop singers, iconoclasts and zealots, of degenerates and Jesus freaks, crackpots and milksops, of psycho groups and motorcycle gangs, of muttonheads and missionaries, refugees and rubber-neckers, savants and visionaries, of rapers and Rosicrucians, of witches and hypnotists, exorcists and scientists, weather prophets and spirit writers, fallen angels and rising stars, Sufis and poets, of all the klepto-, dypso-, pyro-, megalo-, and biblio- maniacs, and of all the wandering minstrels and Jews, gypsies and vagabonds, adventurers and street-beggars, that from all the derelicts, geniuses, outcasts, and academicians, from the half-wits and prodigies, drifters and communards, the drug addicts and book worms, quadriplegics and lost souls, from the whites, blacks,

Chicanos, Indians and Orientals, that from the whole glorious Turkish bazaar of life that is "Berzerkeley," now and then arises a spark in the tinder box, a new movement, kindled usually by some asinine repressive measure, that, flaming up in the receptive brew and fed by the mass media, then flashes across the country like a brush fire, creating new blazes in Madison and Chicago before arriving at the East Coast colleges and youth ghettos where, after a brief eruption, is dampened, tempered, controlled, debated, refined, written out to be sent across the Atlantic to damp London where it sits and smolders for a couple of years before crossing the Channel to Amsterdam, Berlin, Paris, Rome, the entire youth of the Western world enflamed by the little town of Berkeley, California. Of course, by the time the movement arrives in Paris, it is only the tepid ashes of the original conflagration, the surging magma vaporized by the good French *goût*. When the Women's Liberation Movement began, for example, bands of women libbers in Berkeley would lay in wait for men who whistled or pinched the butts of passing females, to which they would respond with a verbal lashing or even a vicious beating, while in Paris, they're simply sending out leaflets demanding that contraception be reimbursed by social security.

Under the desert of the established order of government, university, hospitals, hotels, and supermarkets, there is a whole subterranean oil field of underground institutions riddling the Berkeley community with the steady pumping of its wells, expelling the flatulent evil-smelling gas of an entombed past, like a good cathartic fart, and, at the same time, allowing the energy-rich blood-essence of the population to surge up from the tapped well-heads of the New Age. When the prices in the markets begin to skyrocket, does the Berkeley mob stand in line at the cash registers reading Adam Smith and Keynes? No! In the back room of some vegetarian commune they concoct, to the wail of Jimi Hendrix and Janis Joplin, an incredible plot: the Food Conspiracy! Whole blocks of citizens join together and, at half the price, arrange to buy food wholesale at the old produce market. Berkeleyites do not whine; they just ignore what doesn't suit them, that is to say, everything that they don't create with their own minds and hands. A case of clap? Bad acid trip? Overdose? A stubborn cough? A splinter in the big toe? No need to go the hospital and fill out a thousand forms or, if without money or insurance, to be left to die on the doorstep. No need to go and pay the ridiculous prices of some doctor for the privilege of giving you an aspirin as he rushes to pay off some cracker politician to prevent any sort of government health plan. It's the Free Clinic and their renegade doctors that will care for your ailing body and without paying, without forms. It makes me wonder—here everything is free: Free Church for a little moral support after having run away from parents or mate, or just a place to flop for a couple of nights for those hard up for cash. The Free University where there are no ridiculous grades, neither 'teachers' nor 'students.' Everybody is a teacher and student: if you have a little special skill like caning chairs or repairing bicycles, well, you go to the Free U to share it with those who want to learn, and perhaps there happens to be an expert there in hermetic philosophy, which is something you have just always wanted to know. So, as he expounds on the alchemist's secrets, you try to untangle the awry spokes that he has just tried to replace without too much success.

Wanting to somehow be a part of this crazy community, I decide one day to sign up for some classes at the Free U. It's located in an old, dilapidated house that has been redecorated, mostly with revolutionary and psychedelic posters. Looking for a list of classes, I open a door only to find a room full of people standing on their heads doing yoga; in another, kids are busy strumming funny guitars. I finally find what might be called an 'office,' and I ask some guy there with spacey eyes to give me a list.

"List?" he answers. "There ain't no lists here, man. Just look around on the walls."

He's right. I don't know how I missed them, for here and there, all over, are little slips of paper tacked up like butterflies: "Want to get together with people interested in Zen gardening. Contact Ophelia." Ophelia? Who the hell is Ophelia? Another reads: "Experimenting with peyote. Let's get together and share experiences. Meet here Friday." No date, what Friday? This could have been put up weeks ago. Just above is another: "Want to meet people to discuss revolution. Chinese and Cuban examples especially, perhaps leading to action. Contact Ed at the Red Flag Bookstore." After browsing awhile around the walls, I decide on three: a course on existential philosophy for my mind; one on massage techniques for my body; and, to give society its due, I decide to take part in an anarchist group, the latter being the first to meet.

Having already studied in the 'normal' university the whole gamut of political philosophy, from Plato's *Republic* to Lenin's *State and Revolution*, from Montesquieu's *Spirit of the Laws* to Stirner's *The Ego and His Own*, I came to the conclusion that anarchism, as best exemplified in the philosophy of Proudhon, was the best foundation on which society should be built:

> *The People is nothing but the organic union of wills that are individually free, that can and should voluntarily work together, but abdicate never. Such a union must be sought in the harmony of their interests, not in an artificial centralization, which, far from expressing the collective will, expresses only the antagonisms of individual wills.*

But when I poked my head out of the university and into the real anarchy (as opposed to anarchism) of the society into which I was born, I realized that, given the state of the age, all this was pure utopian dreams; and so, I said, if the ideal is unrealizable, why struggle, why care at all about a society which, like all societies, seems to move and convulse by its own momentum, its own strange laws. All the theories and struggles to change the world, what are they all but man's presumptuousness in face of the unknown; his sorry belief that he can turn the stream of events in his own favor, his use of the lie of the 'common good' in his naked struggle for power, domination, and blood.

A week later, as I climb the stairs of the apartment building in which the anarchism meeting is to take place, with thoughts such as these forming in my brain, I cannot really understand why I am even here. It's as if I have to put to use somehow those five years of university, as if somehow those years would otherwise be wasted, when, in fact, as I only later realized, they had served their purpose very well, for besides acquiring a certain discipline of mind, by taking one subject matter to the very limits of thought, I saw that thought itself is limited and that yet all our human institutions are based on this limited thought, that every philosophy ultimately comes down to an irresolvable contradiction, whether it be between authority and liberty in the political context, between society and the individual in the social context, or between the past and the future in the individual context—that in fact all our sacrosanct institutions—country, party, state—are based on ideologies which are themselves but man's puny attempts to rationalize his insatiable desire to profit, dominate, and reap revenge. Millions slaughtered, hacked to death, buried alive—in the name of what? The mistaken belief that man can create something new, the mistaken belief that man is other than the trees and oceans and stars of the cosmos in which he is inextricably enmeshed. Through that miniscule part of himself, which is his thought, man makes of himself a god. He creates a phantom world in his mind and then tries to squeeze and maul and pummel the pulsating, living flesh into this box of thought, only to see it explode all around him as the Cosmic Law of Being exacts its due.

I enter the room where the meeting is to take place. Revolutionary posters cover the walls. Tracts, pamphlets, flyers, magazines, hundreds of books lay around everywhere. No one is here. I look at my watch. It's time. I'm impatient for a second, then I laugh to myself. Of course, I would be the only one on time to a meeting of anarchists. Sitting down on the torn, filthy couch, I remember two years ago at the university, sitting in at the Administration Building, one of a score of us protesting the Vietnam war—out of 25,000! Just sitting there in my righteousness along the wall. People coming and going. Doors opening and closing as usual. Telephones ringing. The footsteps along the hall. God, how I remember the footsteps—like cannon shots! I'd never been so uncomfortable. The looks I got, as though I were some sort of fungus growing on the wall. How idiotic I felt there and yet how conscious I was of everything around me. Thoroughly ill at ease and electrically alive. I just couldn't take it. Without a word to my comrades, guilty as hell, I got up and walked out. It could have happened yesterday, so clear it is now.

Finally, the others begin to straggle in, until there are seven of us sitting haphazardly around the room.

I am at once ready to begin a lively discussion on Proudhon's theory of industrial organization or Kropotkin's conception of mutual aid. Theory before practice I say to myself. But it seems that I am out of step. "Direct Action" is the slogan of the day,

Nechayev is their idol. When they begin to bandy about his name, I start to get a little nervous, for I had studied him well, a 19th century Russian terrorist who had no qualms about executing refractory members of his secret cell. As they praise his methods in increasingly glowing terms, I can only just sit here and hope they like me. I feel a little more at ease when Bakunin's name comes up, that mad revolutionist with his secret organizations, running all over Europe at every hint of uprising or revolt. He's more to my style: no gratuitous assassinations, but rather controlled rebellions intermixed with organized meetings. In any case, this name-dropping lasts about ten minutes before someone shouts:

"Enough talk, let's get down to direct action!"

"All right, what's our target? The government? The bank? The university?"

"What's the difference? It's all the same shit!"

"Right on, brother!"

"Bomb the police station!"

"Assassinate the chancellor!"

"Kidnap the mayor!"

"But," I insist, "how can we take part in any sort of action if we don't decide on a theoretical basis for it? How can I do something if I don't know why I'm doing it?"

They all look at me as if I have just descended from Mars, as if "reasons" are so understood, so "in the air," that nothing need at all be said on the subject—which does not satisfy me in the least. Sticking to my guns, I refuse violent action without theoretical justification and they, being 'anarchists,' cannot force their position on me. Knowing that it will be impossible to find any sort of theoretical agreement among seven intellectuals, the only compromise possible is in the type of action to be perpetuated, that is, something not so violent as to do any real bodily harm. Finally, it is decided to rent a safe-deposit box in a local bank. Three of us are to fix up forged identity papers with which to rent it, three are to do the actual renting, and one is to place in it the human excrement by which the bank is supposed to be closed by the smell. One of the group assures us that the bank has no right to open the box without the consent of the renter. Unfortunately, or perhaps fortunately, we break up, and as good anarchists, we don't fix date for the second meeting in order to put the plot into practice.

*

It seems like everything in Berkeley is like that; nothing ever lasts, a meeting or two, at most three or four, and it all peters out. The class on massage techniques is no exception, but it's understandable given the situation. The first meeting takes place at night in the big front room of an old fraternity house. I am pretty nervous as I walk in and see the huge crowd of people, about half male and half female, nervous because, while I tell myself that massage will be helpful to know, in the back of my mind what I am after is sex—in fact, as I soon find out, that's the reason everybody is there whether they know it or not. In any case, any other pretense is quickly dispelled, for the leader of the class creates such a sensual atmosphere that the mind of the body completely usurps that of the brain. The first thing he does is close the door.

"You never know who may walk in and get the wrong idea," he says smiling.

Everyone is standing around uncomfortably checking each other out. There are obviously some guys who have been to something like this before, because I can see them edging slowly behind the more beautiful women. He then puts candles all around the room and turns off the lights, puts on some music of the sound of the sea on the record player, lights incense and puts bowls of perfumed body oil evenly around the mats that cover the floor. Then without further ado, he says, "Okay, everyone take off your clothes."

Just like that. Well, obviously I'm expecting something of the sort. I mean you don't go to a massage class in Berkeley without expecting to take off your clothes, but, my God, I have never been naked in front of a whole group of strangers before. Some people are just going right at it, as if they are getting ready for bed. Others are moving like in slow motion, caught in too many contradictions. A few others, like me, are just standing there like idiots trying to decide whether to leave or go through with it. Finally, after fitfully trying to find a theory to justify the action, I just say "what the hell" to nobody in particular and take off my clothes. Then it happens. So strange-like, just standing here, me and my body—as if somehow I were not my body—and as if everyone were looking at my body but not at me, when undoubtedly no one is paying any particular attention to me at all. And yet, to take off my clothes is to lay myself bear—no pun intended—but through some inner connection to actually expose that inner self hidden behind my uncontrollable manifestations in the world; as if, for a moment I am forced out of my closet of fear, open now and vulnerable.

All I want is to run out, leave, escape—but my pride won't let me. I am caught vice-like in this horrible contradiction, this terrifying inner struggle, which, more strange yet, is totally oblivious to those around me; a struggle which superficially is between staying or leaving, between courage or cowardice, but which ultimately is a conflict between being and not being—

whether to have or not the courage to be what I really am. Caught, split, torn, unable to accept the simple fact of my own existence—such as I am and in this body—as if to accept such a fact will expose me to destruction, annihilation and death. Just standing here naked, unable to take that one step of self-acceptance which will mean the beginning of a change in being, I, or rather something in me, changes the world. Caught up suddenly in a frightening lucidity, an incredible perspicacity, like a plane rising through the fog to the sunlight above the storm, every detail of every object, every person, becomes as though unclouded, clear, shimmering, little worlds unrelated neither to each other nor to me. The eye of that person there across from me, every lash distinct, every blood vessel incredibly well-defined, an eye perfect in itself, but it does not particularly belong to the face, and yet the face is as though seen under a microscope, every freckle, every wrinkle, perfectly in focus, but it does not particularly belong to a body, yet the body is a body perfect in itself but does not particularly belong to the crowd, and so with all things in my vision, which are right and perfect and razor-sharp but without relation—and everyone is dead! And I look at my hand and it is apart from me, and I look at my foot and this too is strange to my being. I have become pure consciousness, disembodied, without fear, for every person is a thing and "I" am totally stripped of all emotion.

Yes, this is marvelous, I think, so safe in here in my velvet-lined cave, and so lucid. Then I see my body move over to my left where a girl is standing as the voice of the leader booms out as though from inside a barrel, "Now everyone get a partner."

It is just so delicious to ask her without fear to be my partner even if I am a zombie and she made of paper mache. The only trouble is that when we go down on the mats at the direction of the leader, I see that my body acts totally on its own, is totally compliant and horny as hell! It's a good thing she is too, because I don't know what to do when, during a lesson on frontal massage, my hands keep lingering over her breasts, but to which, thank God, she makes no objection. In fact, when I start slapping the body oil on her legs and she starts moving them like greasy pistons, and my hands move up closer and closer to her crotch, I see from that lucid distance where I am that she is beginning to breathe heavily and to make little, round, grinding movements with her hips, all not without a certain pleasure. So far away I am from the whole situation, so unable to control the automatic manifestations of my own body, that I find myself crawling over her about to stick it in right there in front of everybody. At that moment, the thought strikes me that I do have a choice after all. I see at that moment that I can enter my body as well as hers, be one with it, but at the price of the anxiety of being responsible for it as well. Poised above her like a hawk, she in sensual oblivion, I receive an instant of pure insight: I see that I am, in this world, really no more than what my body does, that I am my activity, that my actions define me because they relate to the world and to others. Nothing sentimental or moral here, just the pure cold fact that I am not alone here on this earth. It is not even thought now, just pure realization: I had everything backwards! My world is not my thought, because my thought relates to nothing but itself. My thought of what I am is only dreams and fantasy, while the more I relate to the world, the more I am—and, no doubt about it, what with the sea music pounding in my ears, the incense, the candles flickering around the room, I'm about to relate to this girl right now in front of everybody—and I jump up in a horrible fright!

As I said, the class doesn't take place more than twice, for when the word gets around about what is going on, there is a huge crowd of drooling perverts at the second meeting that scares away all the women. With the women gone, of course, none of the men want to stay either since no one is interested in massage techniques anyway.

*

The massage class, of course, is just another pretext, an intellectual's singles bar for meeting people, finding sex. I can't understand it; as I make these forays, as it were, into life, behind every meeting, every class, every encounter even, it just seems to come down to sex and more sex. All the rest of it: the search for knowledge, political action, the social whirl, all seems to be but one means or another of lying to oneself. All everybody really wants is someone to go to bed with. Me, too! And if that's the game, I'm going to play it to the hilt. So I pick up a woman in a class I took, just like the rest of 'em. End up almost living with her so often am I sleeping at her place. Her real name is Emily, but she calls herself Amelia. She thinks there is something more European about it that way, more refined, she says. She calls me sometimes or sometimes I call her. It makes no difference because I don't really care. She is just somebody to be with. I need her, true, but only because she is the first to have come along after my wife left me and went home to her mother. I first saw her in the class on existential psychology I took at the Free U. I saw her looking at me. I looked back and smiled. Seemed like the natural thing to do. During the break she came over and sat down beside me.

"Why are you taking this class?" she asks with a sort of lecherous smile.

"The subject interests me," I answer stupidly, half believing my own lie, but knowing quite well that if I find a woman to sleep with the class will lose any 'interest' it might have.

"It interests me, too," she continues even more stupidly. "Maybe after class we could get a cup of coffee and talk about it."

"Sure," I say, understanding perfectly that she is inviting me to bed and glad of it, at the same time feeling a sickening disgust at the need we have for each other.

Healthy love, healthy sex, I know intuitively is the result of a fullness that overflows into the other, not this sickly need to be with, to touch, another human being just in order to feel alive. God! Why would anyone take a course in existential psychology anyway unless he feels a lack of existence, a loss of contact with the world around him, a horrible fear of the world and a pride that is more of an alibi saying that he doesn't need the world nor anyone in it. One cipher in the lonely crowd sick unto death of the American dream. We are all there like starving refugees one sees in advertisements demanding money to feed the victims of the latest drought, famine, or war: bones pushing against skin, sunken cheeks, distended bellies, eyes hollow voids without light, a pleading outstretched hand. Only it isn't food we need. We have, or could have, full middle-class stomachs, fat paychecks, stereos, TV's, electric carving knives, automobiles, leisure time, vacations at Yosemite, Carmel or even Hawaii. But we are empty, empty like echoing caverns, black holes sucking our energy into the pit of nothingness, leaving only bat-like squeaks of nervous desperation. I can see it as I look around: the sly glances everyone is giving, the desperate need for recognition is in everybody's eyes. Who is available? Who can I latch on to? Who can I suck dry in order to feel alive, suck into this bottomless spit of mine so as not to suffer alone?

So, it starts like that. After coffee and the preliminary conversation to make the obvious not so obvious, we go to her place where I stay the night. Seems she is a bureaucrat in some government office—lives alone in an apartment in Oakland. Neither of us goes to the class anymore. We got what we wanted out of it: somebody to touch, to have sex with, 'make love,' as they say. It goes on for months like this even if I am allergic to her cat. I don't care for her any more the twentieth time than I do the first, though I can see she is beginning to like me more as time goes on. I can't understand why. After a while I don't even make any pretenses; I just walk in, get undressed and jump into bed, waiting for her to join me. I hardly talk to her. Never take her anywhere, not even to the movie theater which is just down the block. She must be more desperate than I am. She never says a word about my conduct. I guess she sees my indifference and is afraid of losing me, so she starts fixing me huge meals when I come. Sometimes I'll call her first and tell her what I'd like for dinner. It is always waiting for me: steaming hot thick steaks and mashed potatoes, or duck *à l'orange*. The trouble is her ploys work. The whole thing has become such a lie, I just want to break it off, but I can't do it; I feel too guilty for taking so much and giving nothing. I'm trapped. It isn't even the sex she craves. I don't think she ever even comes. The sex is like the food, just something to keep me there, a man to relate to in order to prove to herself that she's a woman.

One night I am thoroughly bored and decide to call her:

"Emily, I'm coming over. Make it beef stew tonight. I don't want you to go out of your way for me."

"Are you sure you wouldn't like boiled lobsters. I could run over to Spengler's and pick them up."

"Well, only if you're sure you want to."

"Yes, yes, don't worry about it. I'll see you in a little while."

"Okay, and while you're there, pick up some of those little shrimps I like so much, you know the ones. We'll make a salad out of them. Oh, and, uh, I think I'll take a taxi if you don't mind picking up the tab. I'm a little short today."

"Sure, that's all right. I just cashed my check. Don't worry about a thing."

I'm in the taxi now sliding through the traffic over the Bay Bridge—and then it happens….I don't understand any of it, but I step right out of a dream: a scale falls away, a veil is lifted, I begin to *see*. I know I am still in the taxi. I see the bridge through the window, like a huge erector set, just like I've always seen it. But now I don't know at all why I am in this taxi. I don't know why I am going over this bridge to see this woman. Here I was, just a second ago, thinking about lobsters and vibrators, and now it doesn't interest me in the least. But it's not that, not that an interest has changed, such as the view of a shapely woman sends one's mind awandering. It's as if I have become aware of a whole personality that I never knew was me, as if I have been living a horrible, horrible lie. Here I am, drawn here and there by sex and food like a goat, and all the time I've created this perfect picture of myself, the wandering intellectual, whose sole interest is high ideas and art. This is a horrible, horrible truth. And the anguish is unbearable. The feeling that I am alone, alone, forever alone, envelopes me in a desperate solitude. I am responsible for me. No one else. So why am I going to see this woman? What's drawing me there? Do I really need someone to make my dinner and empty my testicles? I want to get out and walk. The panic is rising inexorably. I've got to get out and walk. But there's no walking on the bridge, no escape. I open my mouth to speak to the cabbie, something concrete to get me out of my thought that has come back in a rush—but my constricted throat only allows a little squelched gasp.

Something snaps now, cracks in two. I'm floating above myself. Everything is fine again. There is my body down there, there is its contorted mind screaming to itself about lies and murder and death....But here, up here inside this little cloud, everything is fine, so peaceful. Here, nothing can touch me, nothing can affect me. People, trees, trash cans—it's all the same, unreal, without relation or weight. I'm sure a slight gust will send everything floating. Even this bridge with a slight groan and snapping of bolts will soon begin wafting over the bay, and around it will be the dancing skyscrapers drifting with the currents. Now I am free, free like an archangel, floating around the taxi. Down there on the seat, that monster there with his twisted mind and hideous body, his problems, fears, and torments, that is the devil. I am the angel, the angel of love, real love, where all flows into oceans of peace, calm, and tranquility. And now images of happiness come fluttering back like tired little homing pigeons so glad to find their nest....

She appears here, behind the eyelids, surrounded by a pale golden light, like a fading yellow photograph slowly coming to life. Her name is Melody, and I see her walking out of the Junior High School I attended in Los Angeles. I am thirteen years old and it's the happiest day of my life. I dared to call her last night. It took me two hours sweating by the phone before I dared to do it. We talked for an hour about nothing and then I just blurted it out: "Can I walk you home from school tomorrow?" And she said yes! So I skipped my last class to make sure I wouldn't miss her and waited there outside behind a tree. I see her coming out. She's only thirteen, too, and there's something fresh and wanton about her. She's wearing a white blouse and a red jumper with straps that accentuate her budding breasts. I can't believe it! She's looking around a little. She's looking for me! I go up to her and she smiles and says to me, "Oh, there you are. I was hoping you didn't forget." Forget, she says. I didn't even sleep last night thinking about it, but with all the control I can manage I say nonchalantly, "No, of course I didn't forget. Let's go to Tony's and get an ice cream." When she puts her arm in mine I almost faint. I am so happy the whole world glows—especially when through the corner of my eye I notice my best friend and rival Timmy Henderson across the street. I usually walk home with him since he lives down the street from me. I didn't tell him on purpose I wasn't going home with him. I wanted him to see us together. I wanted him to suffer like I suffered whenever I saw them talk together at recess. Besides, I wanted to get even for him beating me in the tether ball tournament two years ago in grammar school. I pretend I don't see him, but I observe his face go slack and a dark scowl form as we turn the corner, and then I don't think about him again, or about anything else for that matter. She starts talking to me about one of her girlfriends and it's a good thing she has a lot to say because I can't speak even if I want to. I just radiate with the joy of her being on my arm and all the kids looking at us walking along together. I buy her an Eskimo Pie at Tony's grocery. I don't have enough change to buy two, so we share it, and I am so utterly conscious of biting into what has just touched her lips that I take long slow bites through the crisp chocolate and the sweet soft give of the vanilla ice cream. Everything shimmers and vibrates as we walk along: the trees, the houses, the telephone poles—as if I had never seen anything before at all!

"Why didn't you ask me sooner to walk me home?" she asks as we near the little nondescript house in which she lives. "I was beginning to think you didn't like me."

"Well, you know, I thought maybe you might refuse or something and I wouldn't like that. And then, uh, I thought maybe you liked Timmy."

"Well, I do like Timmy, but not that way," looking m right in the eye as she says it.

God, all that suffering I've gone through for nothing, I thought, as we stopped in front of her door; God, all that for nothing!

"Can I come in?" I ask hesitantly.

"Sure, nobody's home so we can listen to some records."

We throw our books down in a corner chair. I sit down on the sofa while she goes into the kitchen and gets us a couple of cokes. I'm in such a trance that when she comes back into the room it's like an electric shock, as though I am just seeing her for the first time. She is so beautiful and she is alone just with me! I must have imagined this scene every day for the last year. I have such an ache for her, such a longing, but I don't know what to do, how to act. I ask her to sit on my lap, but she plays coquette and refuses. But I have to touch her. I just have to. So I go to the record player and put on Johnny Mathis. He is her favorite at the moment and I put on a whole stack. I don't even ask her if she wants to dance. I can't risk a refusal. If she says no, I'll explode from frustration. I just put both my arms around her waist and draw her to me. I don't say a word and neither does she. She just puts her arms around my neck and for two straight hours we dance like that, in Heaven, hardly moving at all—until her old lady comes home screaming "What the hell is going on? You're too young for this sort of thing," and other such crap.

It was such a paradise I lived that day, that I didn't do any schoolwork for a week. I just kept reliving it moment by moment in my mind until it was burned into my cortex, the memory of that day being more important, strangely, than she was in the flesh. I knew she wanted me to call her. I could tell by the looks she gave me in class, but somehow, by some strange quirk of the mind, to dream that day over and over was more satisfying than trying to go any further with her in reality. It could never be surpassed, ever. So I just relived it again and again in my mind until I didn't know any more what was better, the reality or the dream. Every day for months and months I must have thought about that day: her arms around my neck, her hair against my cheek, the cola on her breath, until by sheer persistence, the dream itself became the reality, and the first stones of a great wall were laid between me and the reality of the world, between me and the Truth....

Another image rises up out of the magma, always the image of Woman and the unutterable attraction, the remembrance of passion and suffering, synonymous words, attraction to life and intensity...The image of Francesca...For every period of my life there is a woman around which everything turns, by which everything takes on meaning. All the rest, school and grades and gangs and jobs and travels, define themselves by the woman I am with or the Woman I am looking for.

But is it really Woman? Or is it the swirling intensity of that one day when I was thirteen years old? Is it that which I am looking for: the intensity, the ecstasy, the furious passion of life that became associated forever that one day with Melody in her little red jumper and her Coca-Cola breath? Something burned and fused in my body that one day, from the marrow of my bones to the outer flesh, something that is mine forever because it is locked for eternity in every cell of my body. Someday I may even forget all the details. I may even forget who was singing on the record player, what she was wearing, even her name, but still I will be looking, searching for that sensation of life that I experienced then, for I touched something within and without far beyond whatever my puny mind may have happened to store away in an image or a word, something in me that touched and was touched by the very source of life and will forever be a part of my being. And if, like a lemming falling off a cliff into the sea, I drown myself again and again in a woman's arms, it is because in her and through her I have more than once touched that vital current, invisible but present, that unites me with the universe itself....

The image of Francesca....I'm sixteen years old and all the purity of that extraordinary day has turned into a scorching lust for my high school sweetheart.

If at thirteen I learned of ecstasy, at sixteen I learned what it meant to love, suffer, and bleed all at the same time. No one day remains now in my mind of my year with Francesca. Most of it has been banished to some secret hideaway in the mind, forever lost to memory. Just the image of her face rises up, the voluptuous lips, the smooth brown skin, the tantalizing shape of her breasts inside a purple angora sweater. Just little vignettes, little sketches, remain now, fading sparks of a once exploding passion. How it started and why it ended I only recall in part, only that certain scenes appear now into consciousness as the taxi nears the end of the bridge and the outstretched hand of the transvestite in the toll booth....

There is a punch bowl filled with a red liquid swimming with orange slices and ice cubes. I ladle out a cup for myself. I am wearing my club jacket, dark blue with "Tigers" emblazoned on the back in white letters. She is standing there by herself sipping out of a cup while she tries to spit out some seeds. She is beautiful and dark, something mysterious and alluring, part Mexican, the other half French I discover only later. Because she is alone and is a little ridiculous spitting seeds out of her mouth and because the punch is laced through and through with rum and gin, and I am feeling a little giddy, I dare to say a few words to her. Seems she wants to talk, too, and before long, much to my surprise, we are engaged in a serious conversation over the various merits of the different gangs and clubs to which more or less everybody belongs to in school. She has just been accepted into one of the girl clubs, the Deltas, which encourages me even more, because they are known to be looser than the others, to not object if at the drive-in your hands stray inside their blouses or up their thigh. Pretty soon we're dancing. The lights are dim, the music slow, and just like that she lays her whole body right up against me, which sets my heart to pounding, my knees to shaking, and my skin to sweating horribly, but which seems like the most natural thing in the world to her even though we've just met. I don't have my car, so I can't drive her home. Nothing to do but ask her if she'd like to go to a movie next Friday night.

"Sure, I'd love to," she says. And so it began.

A little grey couch, a TV, a couple of chairs and a brown rug. This is the miniscule living room in the house where she lives with her parents in the poor East Side of L.A. They both work and this is where we kiss and embrace each other for hours on end after school. Now I'm on the floor with me on top of her. For some reason I'm afraid to talk about sex. It's just not something you talk about when you're sixteen and in love, and we go on and on grinding against each other with our clothes on until my pants are wet and sticky. It goes on like this day after day, week after week, month after month, until one afternoon we get into an argument about something or other and she says she doesn't want to see me anymore. "You've never even asked me to go steady!" she screams, managing to slam the car door on her finger which will entail an operation later on. So that's it, she wants to go steady, give her a ring or something—proof!

Now I don't understand anything at all. I love her like you can only be in love at sixteen and, like that, I just let her go. She wants me to ask her to go steady but instead I just don't see her anymore, like a zombie I let her go because that's what she said she wanted even though I know she didn't want that at all. All I have to do is ask her she's still mine, but instead I drive by her house furtively at night like a sick one every chance I get, suffering horribly the pang of my loss, hoping to 'accidentally' see her without the foggiest idea of what I would say to her if I did.

Suffering masochistically, I relive my experiences with her, daydreaming again and again about those exquisite moments up on Mulholland Drive overlooking the city, when my hand slipped down her blouse for the first time, for example. I begin to love my suffering; I begin to love my suffering more than I ever really loved her. I begin to get an exquisite enjoyment out of my daydreams of what had passed between us and my fantasies of what I would have done 'only if...'. I begin to find my mind, my imagination, a much more pleasant place to be than the real world which I can't control and where I never seem to know what to do....

After a while she starts going with one of my friends in the Tigers and when our gang gets together at the drive-in restaurant at midnight to show off our cars and brag about how far we got with our dates that night, he goes on and on in precise detail about how he took off her bra played with her breasts and got his hand in her pants, and so on and so forth. I pretend I don't give a damn. Like it is an old story what happened between us, an old story finished long ago. But then I would daydream for days on end about what he recounted, how she must have sighed and screamed and wriggled with him like I knew she did. By the time I've gone over it like that for the hundredth time, I am in such delicious pain of jealousy and suffering, I jump into my car and drive for hours on the L.A. freeways, radio blasting, always ending up driving by her house sobbing and weeping. With Francesca I learned so well to love my suffering that I drove another deep wedge between me and the real world, a wedge so deep that something was beginning to crack....

The taxi is snaking through the streets of Berkeley. Stop and go. Stop and go. Horns honking, brakes screeching, sirens whining. But up here, here in the air-tight capsule of my mind, not a whisper, not a rustle, not even a creak. Just another image wells up enclosed in a bubble: the long blonde hair of a woman named Barbara....

She is sitting in front of me in a philosophy class at the university while I'm reading a paper on why none of us in the class can talk without biting each other's head off, which was very understandable given the political polarization in the country at the time. A very philosophical paper it was at that: about world views and existentialism, and how everyone is misunderstood due to viewpoints based on a different weltanschauung, *etc., etc. When the paper was finished and the prof asked for comments, she praised my paper to the skies, said I would be a writer some day or some idiotic thing like that. She was beautiful like an angel, and so after class I went up to her and asked her if she really liked it, then one thing led to another and pretty soon I was in her apartment having tea and biscuits. She lived alone with her eight-year-old son. She must have been at least ten years older than me, which added even more charm to the occasion.*

After that we began to sit next to each other in class, losing interest rapidly in Sartre, Husserl, Jaspers and Marcel. Then we moved to the back row and started rubbing knees. It was just too exasperating, getting rutty like that every Tuesday and Thursday from 10:00 to 11:00. I tried to figure out some way or another of getting her alone, but she always had her kid with her, didn't believe in babysitters. "The kid lost his father when we divorced," she told me, "and he's going to have his mother all the time." Very noble on her part, the poor kid. Finally, I invited them one day to my cottage. I said to her: "Why don't you and your son (I emphasized the word son) come to my place on Sunday. We can have a picnic on the dock." She was delighted and it was quickly settled: I would make the sandwiches and she would bring the potato salad.

I had rented a marvelous little cottage on the lakeshore. Marvelous, that is, in the summer when the weather was hot. In the winter, when it was ten below, the freezing, air would seep in through the cracks and freeze my feet, ankles, calves, and thighs; while at the same time, the heater would send up huge clouds of smoky fumes so that I would sweat buckets from the waist up. I had to wear five pairs of socks and thermal long johns, while above the waist a T-shirt was too much. I'm surprised I didn't die from double pneumonia.

Still, I loved my little cottage. It consisted of three rooms: one in back just big enough for a wall-to-wall mattress, one in front, half the size, where I put an overstuffed chair, a table, two stools and a TV, and on the side was the kitchen. Nothing much for sure, but I loved where it was: far from the hurly-burly of the university, from the strikes, the riots, the marches against war, racism, fascism, and cops. It was in the back of a big wooden, brown-bricked manor along with three others on my right and left. It was on the shore of a lake that separated me from the university, a big lake, and a small dingy came with the cottage. The neighbor on my right was a retired plumber who did nothing all day but fish and drink cheap gin. His teeth looked like a checkerboard. Sometimes he lent me his small outboard motor. Sticking it to my boat, I would tour the lake like a grand explorer, checking out every bay and cove.

What dreamy days I had getting into the boat and rowing out to the middle of the lake, a sultry hot day in early autumn, where the thick humid air surrounded me like insulating foam. The university buildings in the distance were just bare outlines, stabs of shadow and light through the heavy mist, while houses along the other shore melted into the vegetation, the vegetation itself dissolving into the lake, and the lake indistinguishable from the sky. Laying there in the bottom of the drifting boat with the waves softly lapping, looking up at the clouds and hearing a train whistle or siren afar off, I felt the world had stopped somehow. If I picked up a book to study, which I always brought to assuage my guilt on these occasions, they always appeared to be meaningless connections of unrelated words and I never got beyond a sentence or two. I just lay there, lay there like a floating seal, breathing the wet air, exchanging chemicals with the living world....

The day she came was just one of those days. The lake was a miasma with streams of vapors rising from the surface. She was wearing a light flowered dress and carrying a basket. Like Little Bo-Peep. Her son came running up asking what kind of sandwiches I made. When I said peanut butter and jelly, he grinned and I felt good. I showed her the cottage. Neither of us felt like talking and nothing much was said: the air was too heavy. Then we went to the dock and spread out the picnic in the sultry air. We ate everything slowly. The wine took all afternoon. It is hard to say what we did there. We hardly talked. As if we didn't need to. The kid went playing on the shore and eventually I found myself dozing, my head in her lap. As the sun went down strange shapes formed over the water. We went for a walk along the shore. As night fell, we went inside. The kid wanted to see something on TV. So we watched it. Then he said he was hungry. So we fixed up a little dinner. Pretty soon it was too late for them to take a bus back. I invited them to sleep there. She thanked me and said of course. We got into bed. The three of us. I was in the middle. I felt her flesh next to me. The tension was unbearable, but what could I do? The kid was there. She turns to me and whispers in my ear: "I want to make love with you." I say, "I'm not used to making love in front of someone's kid." He must have heard me. The kid says, "I'll go in the other room and sleep on the floor." I can't believe it. I tell him where to get a sleeping bag. We make love in the heat and it is good.

It was like coming out of a coma only to have amnesia: Ten bucks? What for? Slowly, I come to. I realize where I am and where I am going and a huge wave of revulsion spreads over my body. From the taxi I can see her through the window setting the table, the lobsters boiling on the stove, the salad bowl overflowing on the table. It's all I can do not to vomit. I decide to tell the driver to move on with a surge of joy, only to immediately realize that I don't have any money to pay him. Oh, shit! I tell him to wait as I go up to the door.

"The taxi's ten bucks," I say looking at the ground.

She goes to her purse and comes back with a ten spot which she hands to me with a big kiss that I don't return. I don't even say thank you. I just slowly walk up to the driver, head hanging, and hand him the money. Then, like a trapped and beaten dog, I turn around and walk back into my cage.

I don't say a word as I eat. I don't even taste the food. I just hunch over my plate and feel this huge ball of rage growing in my chest.

"You're pretty sociable tonight. What's eating you?" she says.

"What the hell's it to you?" I mumble, juice streaming out of the corner of my mouth.

"Well, what did I do to deserve that?" she says with a hurt expression on her face which only makes me madder. I'm at the boiling point.

"I'd better not talk about it. Very good food," I say, stuffing some lettuce in my mouth.

"Well! You've got your nerve! I go to all this trouble to fix you dinner and all I get are insults, and then only to see you gobble it down like a pig."

I freeze. For a good ten seconds I rest motionless, the fork halfway to my mouth. Then slowly and carefully I place it on the table. I pick up the napkin and wipe the juice off my face. I know at this moment I am perfectly capable of picking up the salad bowl and plopping it on her head, which I almost do. But with all the lucidity I can muster, which isn't much, I keep telling myself, 'It isn't her fault, it isn't her fault.'

The anger bubbles there, like lava on the lip of a crater, with too much gurgling underneath for it to sink back. The only question is whether it is going to explode in a shower of rocks or flow slowly down the sides burning everything in its path. Jaw set, the words come out steel-hard, my body like an iron rod.

"Why do you do it, Emily," I say looking at her right in the eye. "Why do you make me dinner all the time, give me money for the taxi, do everything for me, when all I do is treat you like shit?"

It is a cruel thing to say, true, but it's the only way to get down to the truth of the relationship. Besides, it's either that or the salad bowl.

She just looks at me then, her eyes wide for what seems like an eternity. Then she hangs her head and I can hear little quiet sobs as tears start flowing down her cheeks. I want to kill her. The least she can do is put up a fight, curse me up and down, throw things at me. No, in her own stupid intuitive way she gets to me right where I'm most vulnerable: my guilt. I want to comfort her and kill her all at the same time which only exasperates me further. I think I am going to have an apoplectic fit. I start screaming at her. The more I scream, the harder she cries. The harder she cries, the more guilty I become. The more guilty I become, the harder I scream.

"But why do you do it? Why? You know it's all a damn lie! You know I don't really care. You must know! I never take you anywhere. What do I do when I come over to see you? Eat and screw, eat and screw, that's all! How do you take it? I hardly even talk to you. I don't even want to talk to you. There's nothing to say. I suppose you'd like me to say sweet nothings in your ear. Really, all I want to do is come. Physical pleasure without an ounce of feeling. It's horrible. I can't stand it anymore. You hear me! I can't stand it anymore!...Well, why don't you ever tell me off? Tell me to leave, get lost? Why do you keep me? I'm not worth it. I treat you like shit, and you never seem to give a damn. What are you, some kind of masochist? Well, stop whimpering and say something, damn it!"

We just sit there for a while listening to the faucet drip.

"What do you want me to say?" she finally responds almost inaudibly, in a hoarse whisper, "I needed you. I still need you."

"Oh, my God, have you no self-respect, Emily, and besides what do you mean you need me? You don't need me. You need a man and I happened to come along. Any man would have done as well as long as he could get it up. The rest of it is only a lie that you tell yourself so you don't feel like a whore. You don't really care for me any more than I care for you. You needed some human contact, preferably below the waist, and so did I. So here we are. Why don't we just admit it at least? We don't need each other at all. What we need is sex. Or at least that's what we think we need. What we probably need is to find out why we go to such lengths, lying and the rest of it, just in order to join these two organs together."

"Now just wait a damn minute. If our relationship is all such a lie and I'm no more than a whore in disguise, why do you keep coming. It was you who called me tonight, remember?"

"Okay, *touché*," I say more calmly. "I suppose I haven't broken it off because I felt I was taking advantage of you. Come to think of it, I suppose the reason I treat you so bad is just because I keep hoping you'll tell me to get lost so I don't have to say it to you!"

"So, you see me because you think you're doing me a favor, huh? Whew! You really are a complicated sicky, aren't you? Look, maybe you're right, maybe it's true I just needed a little human contact, a man to put my arms around. What's wrong with that anyway? What do you expect from a relationship, to be transported into another world or something?"

"Emily, a relationship shouldn't be based on this sickly need we have for each other. It's disgusting and weak. The longer it goes on the more I hate myself. It must be the same for you if you'd only stop lying to yourself. One minute you rationalize the situation by saying to yourself that you love me, then the next minute you realize how indifferent I am that hurts your pride, so then you tell yourself that it's all for sex, which is perfectly all right, too, and you go out and buy a vibrator. It's all lies, lies and more lies!"

"Well, you answer me, then. What is a relationship for, what do you want? I'll tell you what you want! You want to be madly and hopelessly in love like some idiotically romantic adolescent who just had his first wet dream. You think sex without passion is some sort of sin. Your morality makes me puke! Not to mention the hypocrisy of coming over here and sharing my bed all the while! You're a walking lie yourself!"

"I know it, damn it! That's what I'm saying! That's why we've got to break it off. The only way we keep it going is to lie to ourselves, to hide the desperate need we have for a relationship, any relationship, with another human being. It's the solitude that's unbearable. Why it's so horrible to be alone, I don't know, but that's the way it is. Finally, we get so desperate we just change the reality of things to suit our idea of what *ought* to be. Your idea of a couple comes from your past experience and my idea from mine. If what we have doesn't match up, presto, we imagine it to be what it isn't. You'd be surprised what I'm capable of that way, imagining things different than what they are. I remember when I was living in L.A.; you know what a desert that place is, driving from suburb to suburb for hours just to run an errand: block after block of gas stations, plastic pizza parlors and banks. I would pretend I was in Paris, Naples, Rio, or even Bali, places I had read about and was dying to see. Can you guess the power of imagination it would take to change Ventura Boulevard into the Champs Elysée, the Harbor Freeway into the route along the Amalfi coast? I've become such an expert at changing the world in my mind anything becomes possible. To get back to the point, the other day I met this girl in a bookstore. I was desperate for a woman. Whenever I'm desperate, you know, I wander into bookstores. Anyway, there she was looking at this book in the philosophy section. It was Zarathustra! We started talking. About Nietzsche, Goethe, Thomas Mann and what not. I invited her for coffee. We must have sat there talking for five hours nonstop. I was already madly in love with her after the first five minutes! Just what I was looking for, the princess of my dreams: intelligence, looks, etc., when all of a sudden, after these hours and hours of jabbering, there's a break in the conversation. The night before, my roommate and I went barhopping, looking for women. Didn't find any either, which probably had something to do with it. Anyway, I didn't get more than three hours sleep. So here we are, five straight hours of talking, face to face, when bam! silence. I'm just looking at her and I realize all at once that I'm totally exhausted and all tensed up. I half-intentionally relax my body, and I just can't believe what I see. Sitting in front of me is this homely creature who can't believe the fact that anybody thought enough of her to spend five hours in conversation actually listening to what she had to say; and what she had to say, I realized at the same time, was no more than sentimental dribble and words filched straight from a textbook she had undoubtedly been studying for some exam. I could just see it in her face: she was sure I was going to ask her out, maybe even take her to bed, which was all she wanted, a dream come true, a man interested in her! And me, I just sat there stupefied. I couldn't believe it! How did I lie to myself like that? How could I have taken things so far from the truth? Where does this incredible desire to deceive myself come from?"

"So, what did you do?"

"Well, of course, I felt guilty as hell because all I wanted to do now was split. There was no way to do it gracefully. After all that enthusiasm, you just can't say good-bye and walk out. So, I excused myself saying I had to go to the bathroom and snuck out the back door. What else could I do?"

"Yes, just like you, the cowardly way out. Maybe if you had asked her out, even if she was a boring waste of time, given your romantic fantasies, that is, you might have given yourself a little lesson on being more honest with yourself. Did you ever think of that? To bear for once the responsibility of your acts, no matter what lies you tell yourself? No, that would be too much of an effort for you, wouldn't it? Anyway, I get the message. You win. I'll say it for you since you don't have the guts: Get out! I never want to see you again. Is that clear enough and straight enough to the point for you? Or would you like me to write it in blood attached to a lie detector?"

"No, no, I didn't mean that…"

"Oh, okay, then, let's go to bed."

"No, uh, well, I did mean that, only…"

"Only what?! Only what?! So guilty, just like a little boy. Why don't you just get up and leave, Michael, before you die of indecision."

I half look at her with a sickly smile, get up and walk out the door.

*

In Berkeley, sex and politics definitely go together, as they do everywhere. In any case, I have a friend there, Jim, whom I met at the university back East where I got my graduate degree. An intellectual radical he is, not afraid of putting his ideas into action. He came to Berkeley supposedly to do some research for his thesis, but like all the radicals, he was just drawn there like a comet to the sun. What with his mustache, the fiery glint in his eye, the continual diatribe against 'relativists,' I have the impression when we're together of being with the reincarnation of Trotsky himself. He lives with his girlfriend, Sherry, in a cracker box that isn't worth ten dollars rent, but for which they pay some exorbitant amount for the privilege of listening to the rats, screaming and love-gaspings of the neighbors. Along with the rest of their apartment house composed of students, drop-outs, and workers, they are part of a rent strike sweeping the town. One of their neighbors, a black guy who visits them, likes to twirl his revolver in tune to Santana saying, "Man, if that fuckin' honky comes at mah door to get his green, he's gonna get a silvah bullet 'tween his fat white cheeks."

One evening engrossed in the sexual divagations of Henry Miller, I get a call from Jim:

"Hey, man, you've gotta make it over here. There's gonna be some action tonight."

"Yeah? What sort of action?"

"Retaliation. The pigs've been hasslin' the people 'bout dope, you know, raids and shit like that, but only the rent-strikers by some funny coincidence. The people are gettin' it together all over town. I've been in meetings all day, organizing guerilla bands. It's all set up."

"Okay, sure, sure, I'll be right over. See ya later."

As I stand outside my flat trying to hitch a ride, I try to think of a good reason for getting myself involved: participatory democracy? direct action? power to the people? They all seem hollow as gourds, so I just keep repeating stupidly to myself a phrase from Rimbaud: "You do not know where you are going, or why you are going. Go in anywhere. Answer everything. They will not kill you any more than if you were a dead body." '...Go in anywhere....they will not kill you...answer everything... they will not kill you...they will not kill you...'

I'm picked up by a couple of students at the university. They're in good spirits having just made a good deal on some bennies which they're going to use to stay up all night studying for a test in sociology. I recount to them what Jim has told me about the impending street action, but they don't seem to be interested wrapped up as they are in the numerous theories they keep bouncing off one another in preparation for their exam.

When I arrive at Jim's apartment, the place is a hubbub of activity. Jim is in his own, typing up furiously some message he whips to someone slipping out the door, shouting hortatory speeches to lackluster spirits, execrating tergiversates who have wandered from the correct revolutionary punctilio. When he sees me, he jumps up with light streaming from his eyes.

"Oh, Mike, you're here! It's gonna be a fine, fine night tonight! We're all organized, organized, the town's covered; we got guerrillas downtown, guerrillas uptown, guerrillas at the university, guerrillas everywhere! You remember the strike at U. of W., how we made 'em call out the National Guard just to keep the school runnin'? Well, tonight, man, they're gonna have to call out the whole fuckin' army just to keep this town on the map. You just stick with me tonight, baby, hear? 'Cause the revolution starts tonight, tonight! Oh, yeah, it's gonna be a fine, fine night tonight!"

And like a stunned whore he kisses me on the mouth. When we step outside the crisp air of the deep, blue night sends electric bumps up and down my spine. All the smog and dusty debris has been swept clean by a cool breeze from the sea, and a luminescent sheet of stars covers the city. Jim gives a couple of last orders to hangers-on:

"Tell B-Group to stay off the Avenue! Off the Avenue! A-Group's to hit the banks! The banks! No beauty parlors, hear?!" And we walk together alone towards the university.

"It's like Che said," he explains to me feverishly. "we're in the belly of the beast, the beast! And we're the divine cancer gnawing the slime covered capitalist innards. We've gotta

146

break on through, make an incision, cut through the propaganda, let the blood flow out, man!"

"Yeah, sure," I say looking at him a bit sideways.

"Oh, you know me, Mike," he responds in quite another tone. "I'm not so innocent as all that. But we've gotta start somewhere lettin' people know there's somethin' else except makin' money. Shit, I know there's not gonna be any revolution tonight—break some windows, chase pigs, choke on some gas, and tomorrow it'll be all the same—except for those there in the street, man, because once you've tasted the street and then try to get back inside, well, man, then it smells just like a ten-ton turd. I don't see how they do it, some of 'em, today smashin' windows and tomorrow linin' up for a job, and in a year workin' in some office. They've gotta know they've copped out! They've gotta! They've gotta! It feels too damn good being free!"

We reach Telegraph Avenue and start walking up the street past that strange conglomeration of chic boutiques, head shops, plastic pizza parlors and dusty bookstores.

"Look at that," Jim says pointing to a square block of asphalt and close-cut grass. "Two years ago that was People's Park. People lived there. They ate, they drank, they made love, they played with the kiddies. It was like home 'cause they made it themselves. You think they called out the National Guard, gas-bombed the city, cracked heads because somebody forgot to get a permit. Ha! It was because the people they were supposed to govern or give an education to didn't have any use for those bastards sitting behind their titles and uniforms. It wasn't the law they were trying to uphold, but their own fucking self-importance."

We're just about at the university now and, looking around, something feels missing. Of course! There are no street peddlers or beggars, but I do notice that little groups of people are everywhere just hanging out. It's evident something's up. The tension stretches over the city like wires.

Then, from a distance, comes what is to be the familiar sound of breaking glass. Again and again. Soon a band of about twenty comes streaming around the corner popping streetlights with rocks.

"Come on! Let's go!" Jim screams as he dashes to join the group. What can I do? So I trot along behind him. The wail of sirens is ever present in our ears when we reach a huge group gathered at Sproul Plaza at the entrance to the university. Some in front are laughing and making cute, insulting remarks to the police. The Stones' *Street Fighting Man* is blaring out of an apartment house window. Some start dancing while others start looking for thick throwing things. Couples play feelies on the outskirts under trees. Joints are handed around like peppermint sticks. Jim starts organizing rocks in people's hands. Sherry too. The cats meow and the air is cracked with rhythmic chants: "Power to the people! Power to the people! Burn! Burn! Porkchops! Porkchops! Burn! Burn!"

There must be about 2,000 of us facing two hundred mighty nervous cops in helmets and boots and leather and black and big batons. Some real fat cop picks up his visor and through puffy cheeks begins announcing like an automaton through a loudspeaker:

"By Law 546 of the penal code as enacted September 4, 1956, by the people of California..."

"We're the people! We're the people!" all the kids scream in unison.

"...illegal assembly."

And the mood changes like channels and the rocks fly and police charge and Jim is working away like a warm-up pitcher. "Got 'em, the bastard!" A bearded Christ comes up with a beatific smile, "Peace, brother, a little love." Jim hands him a fat rock in the groin. Clubs come down hard on heads. Thwat! Crack! The people's medics and the pigs fight over the injured. People are running everywhere chasing or escaping. I don't know what to do. Jim hands me a rock. "Throw it, damn it!" A huge, visored cop is coming right at me, baton held high. I look at the rock, the cop, the rock...the rock... *(strange these blue flecks.. and here...this little bump making a nose...is it igneous, bituminous?)* "Come on! Come on! What's the matter with you?!" Jim and Sherry pull me by the hand through the mob and screams. "Hit it!" and we start running like track stars with the rest down the street. Plow! A staccato of gunfire and a wall of gas. We turn left someone screaming "Downtown! Downtown!" We come out of the side street straight on to the boulevard lined with shiny shops and big glass windows. Groups of ten and twenty are running up and down dodging cop cars on sidewalks, smashing up store windows like lake ice in spring. "The banks! The banks!" Jim screams to everyone he meets. "Right on, brother!" Crash! Tinkle! "These idiots!" Jim yells as he shoves another brick through plate glass. "They've lost their cool! This place is too spacey to organize! Everybody's stoned out of their skull!" A gas grenade lands two feet in front of us. Cops start flowing up the Boulevard. Helicopters spray gas over the whole city. The groups start breaking up. "We've got to get to Albert's! Let's go!" Choking and crying, we put wet handkerchiefs over our faces and feel our way by alleys through the gas and smoke until we reach the student ghetto and one of the streets lined with old patrician houses divided up into miniscule studios. People on both ends of the street are building barricades and we pitch in like crazy in the dark street. I am glad to do something, and I pick up everything I see and throw it on the pile. Somebody hijacks a bus and sticks it right across the street and lets the air out of the tires. At the other end kids are chopping down trees. Somebody shouts "Pigs!" and the barricades are torched into a huge wall of flame which firemen put out at once from the hydrant and the cops start marching in wedge formation down the street clearing their way with gas grenades and all the kids split inside leaving the street to the uniforms and the stupid moon.

It's all over now and we know it. We close the curtains, bolt the door, push all the furniture up against it, and wait.

"You think they'll try to bust in?" Sherry asks. She looks marvelous with her pink cheeks and these little beads of sweat on her upper lip.

"I wouldn't doubt it," Jim responds, "those bastards are just itching to crack our heads."

We are about fifteen standing around swapping experiences when someone shouts, "Turn off the lights!" And in the dark we feel like trapped rats, and we decide that if they break through the front, we'll head through the back garden and split up, each for himself. I begin to get scared shitless. On the street I didn't have any time, but in here waiting and waiting...I peek through the curtain and sure enough they're charging up the apartment houses, some little prick informer pointing out which ones. Albert is a well-known organizer and we are about to head out the back when they break in from both doors, and when I see they aren't going to break open our heads, I'm glad 'cause it's over.

"All right, you kids've had your fun. Now it's our turn. Where you been all night?" one cop asks, lifting Albert off the floor by his shirt. I can't believe it when I hear him say, "Get your fuckin' hands off me, pig. What does it look like? We've been havin' a party."

"Very cute," says the cop and sends him flying into the corner where he sort of crumples like a slit duck.

"All right, let's go, all of you." And they herd us into a police van, not without a few painful shoves with the end of their clubs.

They keep us down at the station until the morning interrogating us one at a time. It is understood by all of us that we were at Albert's all night and despite threats and promises of leniency and other such bullshit, nobody squeals and in the morning they let us go.

We all go together to a pancake house and I order a huge buttermilk stack about a foot high topped with huge gobs of butter and maple syrup and strawberry jam and nothing ever tasted so good in my whole life. Nobody says anything for a long time being so hungry and so glad to eat pancakes and drink steaming cups of hot coffee.

Finally, Jim turns to Albert and says, "You know, if we just would have made some alliance with the workers, we might have really accomplished something. We're just too isolated."

"Workers, shmerkers," Albert responds sardonically, "the whole thing was maybe a good high and a nice rush, but violence can't go anywhere, and it never will. We've got to wait for an economic crisis and meanwhile do what we can within the system, change it little by little. Nobody out there is going to give a damn about anything as long as their stomach is full and their TV works."

For some reason, I become hypnotized by the melted butter and syrup slowly flowing over the pancakes. The voices are as if echoing around me. I feel alone, like in a drum.

"Bullshit! Maybe you can wait for economic crisis, but not me!" Jim's cheeks become flushed and his hands are trembling. "It's we who have to make the crises! You make enough little mini-actions like last night and people get nervous, they demand order, then more repression, which brings in more people ready to fight, another action, more repression, the spiral grows, things polarize. We've got to follow last night's action up with something soon, or, yeah, you're right, then it will have been just a damn good high."

The butter and syrup are mingling now, making rather strange viscous designs.

"That sounds good," Albert answers getting a little hot himself, "but all this theory, which I admit might be quite true and work just as you say, depends on people, people who have to do violence to other people. I simply cannot believe that any end achieved by violent means would not be infected by the violence of those means. What you're really saying is that you want power for your own ends which you see as the good. Of course, the fact that a whole group of people who don't agree with your version of the good must be eliminated, somehow that doesn't bother you. And, of course, you can't eliminate them all, and so even if you do gain power, they will still be there waiting to slit your throat given half the chance. So you have to keep the lid on, create a police state, always talking about the paradise to come. No, man, it's just no good your way. You can't force change. The only thing we can do is constantly try to keep things more human, not for the mass, but for each individual."

With that, Jim explodes, his neck purple, his eyes bulging....

Like sap it flows down the sides in four streams. I begin to notice tiny little bubbles forming in the mixture.

"All that is reformist, relativist bullshit! I'm talking about REVOLUTION! Fundamental change! I'm not talking about changing the rules a little here and there; I'm talking about changing the game! If there's one thing I've learned in this political business, it's that people are the most adaptable, malleable, conformable creatures on this planet. You create a situation and people respond to it. The whole thing may be completely new, but all of a sudden everybody is an expert, taking sides, making theories, and before you know it, they're playing the new game set up by someone else. I'm saying you change the fundamental conditions by which society operates, you change the people at the same time!…"

As it soaks into the pancakes, they become bulgy. They look like slabs of soggy flesh.

"Sure, at first repression is necessary. No one wants to give up their advantages and riches gained, of course, through the exploitation of others. If they do so voluntarily they will be welcomed into the new society, if not, they must be repressed, yes, even eliminated. What are a few lives compared to a new world! Eventually things settle down, people find their place in the new social order, things go on as before, except now with justice, equality and real freedom."

"And mass graves," Albert adds in a disgusted tone.

Reaching bottom, a pool of buttery syrup forms in the plate. I put my finger in it just like a kid. It feels all sticky.

Jim turns to me and asks, "What do you think, Mike? You've always been in favor of direct action, at least you were at the university. What do you think of this relativistic bullshit Albert's trying to dish out to us?"

As I continue to watch my finger stir the syrup, I find myself saying, "I don't know, I don't know at all, Jim, and I'm beginning to think that I don't really care."

LASKY

Over the Golden Gate Bridge to Sausalito. I received a call from Lasky whom I ran into on Eddy Street the other day. We haven't seen each other for a couple of years, ever since I left the university. I'm on my way to meet him, having borrowed George's car for the occasion. It is one of those days when the fog billows through the Golden Gate like a great moving wall of cotton, smothering everything in its path as it rolls in from the sea. As I enter the bridge enshrouded in thick fog, the abrupt change from the previous clarity of the ocean, the city, the hills, the bay, makes me almost giddy, as if something magical has taken place, as if perhaps I'll pop out at the other end in Zambia, Sumatra, or French Guiana. Traveling as I am in this in-between world on the way to my rendezvous, I am filled with a joyous expectation; for with Lasky is associated the supreme pleasure of stretching one's mind to the utmost in the play of dialectic. What a sensuous enjoyment it was with him to take a revolutionary idea and hold it up to the light like an X-ray, examining it inside and out, or like a jeweler who has studied every facet, every angle, of the glorious diamond in front of him so as to discover just precisely where to cut. To come to a new insight, to understand a philosophical idea that had been out of my grasp for months—it was as good as having sex for the first time with a new woman. I began to see, contrary to the snares of woman, however, how ideas in themselves can be a means of liberation, a broadening of one's vision, a release from the psychic pressures enclosing one in one's own personal cage—that is, if the idea is applied to one's own life in the living of it and not kept stored in the mind as a mental formula to be spewed out for an exam. For this, the need must be there, the passion to know, the desperate longing to understand....

At times I would possess an idea like a knight would a woman: protect it, defend it, let nothing soil its purity until it entered me, became part of my life. The most logical rebuttals I would turn aside with scorn and ridicule. "This is the truth," I would say, "why can't you see it?" And of course, Lasky didn't see it, nobody saw it, because it was *my* truth, an idea that I needed at that moment in time, all the scattered confusion of my mind brought together in this hard jewel of an idea which I would grab onto in desperation and stuff in the bottom of my pocket until life once again would pull off my pants and the jewel, now dirty, scratched, and useless, would roll into the gutter, though, to be sure, its emanations had changed something within me.

Lasky had a good mind, I remember, coming to the end of the bridge—methodical, but not without breadth. What seemed to be missing in him was the spark, the passion, the desire to keep going beyond what he already knew. When he would come back at me with his rational approach, his outline of the problem, I knew he was right as far as it went in summarizing someone else's thought—but I would never admit it. Until I found *my* truth, I could never believe that anything we said could be the end of the matter. There always seemed to be more to dig for, more to find. How can you define, after all, concepts like existence, democracy, morality, natural law? Abstractions like these only have meaning in terms of one's own experience. Every time I discovered 'my' truth, I simply found a relation between the idea and my own life, and either the idea found its confirmation in my life or it didn't exist, that is to say it was simply parroting someone else's thought and had no real meaning for me at all.

But the professors didn't care about my personal understanding. No, what they wanted was Machiavelli's interpretation, or Aristotle's, or Hume's. Anybody's but mine. *Memorize! Memorize!* It was insane! I graduated *cum laude* and didn't learn a thing except the incredible absurdity of what passes for education in our culture. And, oh yes, lest it be forgotten, I learned very well how to succeed in the world, succeed at the expense of everything that could be called *myself*. It was only when I left this ivy-covered ivory tower that I really began to learn, only when I plunged into life without a life preserver, without any idea of what I was going to do, swimming desperately trying to evade all the eddies and whirlpools that are so pompously called the 'responsibilities of life.'

Across the bridge and out of the fog, the traffic wending its way through the brown hills of Marin until I find myself descending like a drop in a river towards the Sausalito exit on the edge of the Bay. Lasky has only just moved there, which surprised me not a little when he told me of it. Surprised, because Lasky is still associated for me with a certain intellectual revolt against established ideas, ideas—though often unstated—that lay behind the course of events of our crumbling civilization. Together in the university we had developed our insurrection, tearing down everything sacred, everything holy, sitting up till the wee hours at my kitchen table, popping bennies and other pep pills, a pot of hot coffee steaming on the stove, or over countless beers in the student Ratskeller, demolishing one by one, like Hercules, the pillars of Western culture. And now, after only two years, he's living in Sausalito, the haven of the rich, with their hot tubs and encounter groups, the refuge of those who 'made it' and have earned the right to lay back and toy with their bodies and minds. As I go through the town and snake up the hill towards his house, I find myself already forming arguments like in the old days, in order to point out to him the error of his ways.

When he receives me, the first thing I notice is the hair thinning on top and the paunch pushing over his belt, things I didn't take note of the other day. He's aged that's for sure. In his face the lines show signs of bills, appointments, and files from his job as a corporate executive.

"Come on in, come on in, I want to show you something," he says opening the door. "It's something we just bought. Here, take this chair and sit in the middle of the room. Now, don't say anything. Just listen."

He turns something on a tuner that must have a hundred buttons and knobs. An incredible sound fills the room with the music of the Grateful Dead, as if blaring from every part of the room at once. Before I have a chance to say anything, he says, "Quadraphonic! Wadda ya think, huh? You ever heard anything like that before? We got it wholesale. My uncle knows a guy. So wadda ya say? It's somethin' , huh?"

"Yeah, that's real nice," I say, "real nice. What did you pay for it?" not really giving a damn but knowing that that's what he wanted me to ask.

"It cost us nothin', I tell ya, nothin' at all. Just a couple hundred bucks. We got a deal you get once in a lifetime. But you should hear Beethoven on it, it'll blow you through the roof."

"Beethoven? When did you start listening to Beethoven?" I ask in amazement.

"Well, when you get a little older your tastes begin to change. Rock doesn't do much for me anymore. I'm beginning to get a liking for Vivaldi, too."

He moves over to the coffee table and pulls out of a little box a tightly rolled joint. He lights it up and offers it to me.

"Well," I say taking a deep drag, "you haven't outgrown grass anyway."

"Columbian. Best stuff around now, almost like pure hash."

"Doesn't it bother you, smoking dope, I mean, given your position and all. If you ever got picked up, it'd be all over for you, wouldn't it?"

"Well, I haven't copped out completely, you know. I do a little lawyering on the side, defending people picked up for drugs. Since they usually don't have any money, they pay off in grass, hash, LSD or whatever. I'm not about to throw it away and selling it is too risky, so what choice do I have?"

He shrugs his shoulders like he's an innocent bystander of the whole affair, as if the events are beyond his control. I see now that drugs are his last bastion of revolt against the consumer-ridden society into which he is being inexorably sucked. After showing me his color TV, power drill, electric hedge cutter, and outboard motor, I decide to try to get him back to the world of ideas that we knew together in college. The possibility that we have absolutely nothing in common any more fills me for some reason with a horrible dread, as though I have become a mental outlaw banished from the tribe and cannot bear to face the isolation of an exile's life.

"Tom," I say almost imploringly, "I want you to look at this book."

I reach into my jacket pocket and pullout a crumpled collection of yellow, wrinkled pages.

"I was in the Mind Bender, you know, that used bookstore off Market Street downtown. I was walking down the aisle and there was this book on the floor. People were stepping on it, trampling it underfoot, tearing the pages, so I picked it up. You know how I've always liked books; it was like a sin to me. So I picked it up and absentmindedly began to skim through it. It was unbelievable, Tom! I couldn't put it down! I just stood there and for three hours and read the whole thing! It was *The Reign of Quantity and the Sign of the Times* by this Frenchman René Guénon. Everything we used to talk about, all our ideas about the individual and society, the social question, the role of science and technology, the place of religion, everything is made perfectly clear in this one little book. I went up to buy it and the guy just looked at it falling apart and gave it to me...."

"Jesus, you're still thinking about those things?" he responds with a condescending smile, "no wonder you don't have a decent job. Isn't it time you did something? I know the other day you said you were doing a little writing, but you don't really call that a career, do you?"

"What are you talking about?! To hell with that! Just listen to me for once and get your mind off your goddamn gadgets for a second, will you?! You don't even ask me what else the guy wrote. Before, you'd have already been on the way out to buy it!

"Come on, forget your book. Let's get outta here. I got some LSD, sunshine, best around. I know a good spot up on Mt. Tam where we can do it, okay?"

"Okay," I say with a resigned smile, knowing I'm beat, "whatever you say."

We drive into the parking lot halfway up the mountain and begin to walk. I've always enjoyed hiking Mt. Tam, alone or with another. The views are splendid here. You just have to raise your eyes and spread out before you like a banquet is the ocean, the great Pacific, stretching to the horizon in a sweeping blue curve. Sometimes on a clear day, when the sunrays lightly play on the surface like dancing sparks, I see but a huge crinkly sheet of cellophane, unreal, without substance or weight. Or, if the fog and haze diffuse the sun's light into more somber shades of grey and brown and a murky yellow, the surface becomes transparent, and I feel at once the depth, extension, and immensity of the ocean's waters. At such a moment, a great longing mounts in my chest, like bread rising, and plans begin to form, vague plans of travel, of changing things, of letting go.

A slight turn of the head and before me lays San Francisco spreading out from the towering skyscrapers downtown, covering her hills with houses of white frosting. San Francisco! Often in my mind's eye, standing here on the mountain like a prophet, I will see with joy or regret, depending on my humor, all the skyscrapers cracking and tumbling like matchsticks in the earthquake to come. Or, in a more nostalgic mood, I will muse over the different parts of that city that I know and love: the Haight-Ashbury where I live like a sewer rat in my dingy under-ground flat, scurrying out only to grab a cheap meal in a café on Haight Street. The underground life! Very romantic, true, but I suffer it just the same. The Haight is changing now. It has lived off its fame as the birthplace of the Hippies for a long time, all of whom have left for the commune life in the countryside, leaving only blocks of boarded up store fronts, junkies, and a few people like me trying to hold on to the past. Now the new wave of gay young professionals is moving into the neighborhood, restoring the beautiful old Victorian apartment houses, raising the rents, forming neighborhood associations to get rid of the derelicts. In a way I know it has to be, yet in my mind the reality of the neighborhood is what it was, not what it has become, and the change taking place is as frustrating as being woken out of a good dream....North Beach, to where now and then I take with pleasure one of the old twenty-year-old street-cars that they keep in service with rubber bands and glue; street-cars so old that every time the Muni needs a new part they have to machine it themselves. North Beach, where the habitués of the little Italian cafés on upper Grant are also trying to live off the past: all the pseudo-poets of the City hang out there trying to bring back the 50's of Ferlinghetti and Ginsberg. Once I got up enough nerve to send in a manuscript to one of the small publishing houses trying to make a go of it in the area. It was a hundred pages of ravings which I thought was the equivalent to Revelations. I received a hand-written, personalized rejection slip, explaining how they thought it was an 'interesting' effort but that they were too busy right now, etc., etc.....I suppose the only areas of the City that are present and alive are the gay areas of Castro and Polk Streets. The gays are taking over whole areas of the City, forming political groups, organizing campaigns. They even got one of their own elected to the City Council because he was homosexual. Of course, he too was blown away along with the mayor by another nut with a gun. When you walk down Castro Street at night, it's like walking the gauntlet. Your butt is black and blue from the pinches streaking out of doorways. It's beginning to be unnatural not to be homosexual in these areas, which must be a contradiction in terms.

San Francisco! What other city in the world could you have a Gay Parade and a Hooker's Ball without raising the ire of the staid citizens who, after all, pay their taxes and vote, too. They all live in the Sunset and Richmond Districts in their neat little

162

houses with their cute green lawns, but nobody ever pays them any attention because they're always covered over with a thick layer of fog coming in off Ocean Beach....

With all the hills and valleys every neighborhood is like a little village. Nobody bats an eye, whether in Cole Valley or Twin Peaks, if you get up in your pajamas and buy your milk at the grocer's that all seem to be owned by Arabs. Nobody cares what you do here. Not at all. Everyone's doing something weird. Walking down the street is just like being at the circus: you're just as likely to see a juggler as a postman, a clown as a cop. If you picked up San Francisco and put it down next to Kansas City, they'd put a wall around it to keep the joy from spreading. You're free in that city, man, and that's why I love it. You don't have to go anywhere else for a little exotica either: Chinatown, Japantown, and then there's the Mission for a good Mexican meal. Soul food can be found in the Fillmore District. And when you get tired of all the weirdness, you can take a good walk through Golden Gate Park which goes something like fifty blocks from the Haight to the beach, where starting from bongos and sax on Hippie Hill, on through a fortune cookie at the Tea Garden, weaving your way through bicycles and roller skaters, losing yourself in the woods, hitting the museum, enjoying the lakes and keeping clear of the buffalo, eventually you'll find your way to a beer at the Beach Chalet reading Herb Caen and admiring the murals of Labaudt. From there, you can walk around Land's End, along the cliffs towards the Golden Gate. I've taken that walk a score of times and I'm just as ready to do it again. I love the wind as it whips my face with the salt spray, the seals barking below, as I try to keep my balance on the narrow path winding through the cypresses; where everybody you pass offers you a joint with a smile, and that last turn in the trail when bam!, the bridge comes into sight spanning the Gate, and the cargoes, tankers, warships and a thousand sailboats passing under orange steel. I almost pass out each time. I'll never get used to it!

It's not bad if you're rich there either. Old hotels and patrician houses. Even the snobs take the cable cars to the Fairmont and Mark Hopkins on top of Nob Hill. You have to be a track star to walk in San Francisco and your clutch'll go out in a month if you try to drive in this City. Once my brakes went out on Washington Street, on a hill that compares to El Capitan. Had seven people in this tank of a station wagon that I picked up for a song in L.A. It took off, and at the bottom of the hill solid cross traffic. Just turned the wheel into parked cars. Demolished five of 'em and nobody got a scratch. I was pretty proud of myself even if I didn't have any insurance and had to go bankrupt.

Of course, all this is only the exterior! If you really want to know what's happening in San Francisco, you've got to dig a little through the beauty and craziness. There isn't a psychology, philosophy, religion, or sect that doesn't have center, school, newspaper, and temple. Since nobody believes anything anymore, everyone's trying to find something to hold on to—and there's plenty of people to give them what they want. There's a lot of this and a lot of that: from acupuncture and encounter to T'ai Chi and Hasidism. To choose, you'd better look at the fruits. San Francisco is a city of extremes. Outside, everything is bizarre, without connection, but underneath there is to be found a whole network of people building something solid, serious people, preparing for the New Age. Zen, Tantra, Sufi are house-hold words to a growing spiral of people who see no more meaning in the American mania for money, gadgets and show biz. The gurus are coming by planeloads from the East, from Japan, India, and Nepal. In San Francisco there are always people ready to lend an ear to an unknown idea. It's fertile ground for old seeds, seeds that only seem new because even the tares are covered over with amusement parks and parking lots. Walking the sex shows on Broadway or the bum-ridden Tenderloin, it could be the end of the world, the outer darkness, but like the first Christians in dying Rome, a new era is being carefully planted, unseen, ready to bloom in the dying of the night. Like I say, San Francisco is a city of extremes. You've got two choices there and two only: go crazy or find God.

Another twenty degrees to the left and the Bay Bridge carries my eyes from the City as it jumps the Bay in two mighty leaps: San Francisco to Treasure Island and Treasure Island to Oakland. The Bay Bridge is bigger than the Golden Gate, but without the latter's symmetrical purity and grace, a product of the site, but none the less true. The bridges always have scaffolding hanging down from the cables like swings. They're always being painted in an eternal war with the sea wind. There's no end to it; by the time they reach the far end, they have to start over like Sisyphus or Milarepa. The painters must be saints by now.

On the other side of the Bridge, rest Oakland and Berkeley nestled under the hills like a couple of suckling pups. Berkeley, being a university town, is a training ground for San Francisco madness. Anything can happen there and usually does. After the ideas are debated on Telegraph Avenue and Sproul Plaza, they become popularized in long stoned discussions in the flats of San Francisco before spreading across the world like locusts. Oakland, on the other hand, is a typical American city, that is to say, divided into two armed camps, one black, the other white. I used to live in Oakland, in a little studio near Lake Merritt with my first wife. It was handy because my job as a letter carrier was nearby. I liked being near the lake, for on the weekends, with nothing better to do, my ex and I would take a boat and go out in the middle and scream bloody murder at each other, letting the boat drift around in circles....

Swiveling around a bit more, there is another bridge in the distance crossing the Bay from Richmond to Marin. The Bay, meanwhile, is carving roundish coves up to the workers in Crockett and the suburbanites in Tiburon. As I raise my eyes to the Berkeley hills, thoughts flicker of long rides on a motorcycle along the crests, hours and hours, down to the beekeepers in Canyon, over to the delta, to Isleton and Rio Vista, and even up 29 to Napa and the wine country. Faster and faster I would ride, without helmet or jacket, the wind and dust tearing into my flesh, on and on trying to outrun myself, escape what I can't understand....

We walk on, Tom and I, the trail leading us down into a forest of redwoods. We haven't said a word, just enjoying the heat, the views, the silence....Finally, after a while we arrive at a little clearing set off from the road that winds through the hills and valleys. Sitting down on a bench, Tom says to me:

"Here's a little yellow pill for you."

"And you?" I ask.

"I'm going to be your guide. I won't be taking any," he answers.

I'm glad to sit down, being hot, tired, and sweaty. I pop the pill casually into my mouth, then allowing my lassitude to gain the upper hand, I doze off before I'm aware of it....

"What's the matter?" Tom says as I sit down next to him, the words resounding.

I look at him and start laughing. He looks so serious and worried, and I could care less. It's just too much; but I answer him just the same:

"Why nothing's the matter. Should something be the matter?"

"You've been sitting there for over an hour staring around you. Then all of a sudden, you just got up and went over to that car."

"An hour? You must be kidding. In any case, there's nothing the matter."

"Are you sure? Because if you're not all right, we can start going back."

"Why shouldn't I be all right? What's the matter with you? Why can't you leave me alone for Chrissake!"

"Don't get angry. I'm just trying to help. Come on, let's head on back to the car."

"I don't want to go back to the car, damn it! Leave me alone! I was in a marvelous place all by myself and now you've ruined it. Go away!"

"No, no. We've got to go."

"No we don't! Get the hell outta here!" I scream getting up and walking towards the road....

whys everyone tellin me what to do just leave people be leave me be ill find things for myself i can read why always lookin for somethin an answer a woman a reason for bein here to do somethin read em all marx mao locke hegel bakunin stirner hobbes kropotkin proudhoun rousseau rackin my brains to get em straight and the next overturns it no end to systems creeds whats it got to do with me what do i give a damn always seems to be a no to every yes seems each day brings its own rules driftin through life unprincipled donothing always see both sides cant do nothin must be someone like me somewhere everybodys so earnest involved force myself to take a stand join picket lines sittin in a revolutionary skeptic feel like im lyin when i act guilty when i dont wanna tear it all down know i do but what for im gonna die mankinds gonna disappear earth just gonna be a cold iron ball in space just dont believe nothing someone on high lookin down just see men and women drinkin and eatin pissin and shitin sittin and walkin fightin and fuckin shove it in pull it out putput sick of marchin in the streets why do i care bout vietnamese ghetto blacks starvin indians never even talked to one its got somethin to do with me i dont care bout em im doin it for me everything i do is for me must feel guilty bout somethin hypocrisy rules everywhere hypocrisy and compromise so where to go limbo congo tango all a bunch of shit want me to join in absurdity a lie to be honest you gotta rebel to be honest you gotta be radical get into politics join new parties peace and freedom new old left tear it down destroy it monopoly capitalist-imperialism militaryindustrial complex get in the streets from below from the grassroots work in the system change the system outside the system destroy the system what system i wanna know dont see no system no absolutes no limits i know it wanna break out gotta get away gotta start livin been on a security track responsibility so important they say prevents me from livin i know it just tell myself im gonna die whats the difference respect and obey nobody tells me why marchin round shootin guns shinin boots insanity everybodys tellin me nobodys askin me conflict everywhere liberty authority individual society past present lifes a flea market swap today for tomorrow freedom for comfort everywhere i go people want to stifle me put me in institutions school army university corporation nuthouse sacred institutions sick of fillin out forms gotta get rid of this shit stuffed in me twenty years of schoolin and rest of my life tryin to forget it gotta break barriers gotta destroy somethin gotta free myself so many conventions laws codes rites rules nothings natural everybody so screwed up me too a kid reading marriage manuals in the dark park that was me sex such a mystery everything makin me want it big tits all over billboards girls layin it up next to me dancin but so hard to get never dared to ask just ask good girls and bad the good didnt the bad did and me in the back seat my pants sticky she probably wantin it so bad not tellin me so stupid with principles like sex was somethin evil dont know why marry a virgin a hole in the hymen why so jealous always like a womans my property but that's what they want expect two of us against the world dont know why should limit myself to one woman get married for a piece of paper dont know why i cant love everybody i told george i remember the words i will never let a woman lead my life i remember and now runnin round like a headless chicken just to put my cock in a wet hole cant seem to control myself nobody ever told me a thing about it this need this desire why is it such a force everybodys talkin about it always perhaps thats all there is to it just fuck my life away why not i attacked that guy at the party took an upper and jumped him and ran hero coward dont know why always blowin my top screamin and yellin bloody dreams sometimes wanna kill sometimes wanna die some kind of war goin on inside me wanna get rid of myself wanna destroy myself all these germs this shit hangin on me cobwebs and dirt brains gonna burst watchin tv hours and hours kill kill kill every day a fight everybodys against everybody afraid of gettin my ass kicked blacks mexicans whites constant war bikers hotrodders surfers cliques and clubs division competition puttin people down always must be somebody somewhere lookin down and laughin rakin it in make your way and fuck the next guy only way to get ahead make your way fuck over someone else i remember bob searchin the park to roll queers dont know why everybody stealin and robbin muggin five locks on every door alarms buzzer riots lootin in the streets machine guns ratatatatatatatatata city on fire gotta find a road out all insanity absurdity war war war killin bombin people on the other side of the planet fightin in the streets strikes breakin windows chasin pigcops kill em smash it choose a career why which one all the same shit no difference just spend my whole life doing one thing and then die but gotta do somethin make money yeah thats what counts only value around how much are you worth all in dollar signs and stock market quotes buy and sell dollar down dollar a week jobs depend on the credit rate gotta be somethin else just gotta be runnin round lost what to do no reason for nothin get a job get a job shananana turn on tune in drop out poppin pills smokin dope hifidelitystereoquadraphonic electricguitarmusic godgroups shake it move it baby rockfestcommunity holdin handsin countryside communes please please pass the joint long flowing hair handshakes and handjobs congodrums in the park singin drinkin wine find a job a flat a job a flat deliver mail basement homes loadin trucks sleepin with cockroaches oh those battered books find a girl yeah find a girl and make love anywhere everywhere on the beach in the mountains in the shower on the kitchen table like im gonna die on drugs ecstasy beyond ecstasy nude group parties psychogroups so free touch me feel me love me drownin in sugar and chocolate all is smiles and love my brothers and sisters all is gumdrops and sugarplums in this little yellow pill all is free now free free freeeeeeeeeeeeee just gotta take it do it take it do it do it no matter what do it do it desperate oh shit ahhhhhhhhhhhhhhhskwwwwkk whered everybody go this solitude crushin me wanna die never thought for myself couldnt stand to be alone worse than death dont know why now its all i got never seemed to control my life nobody made me do nothin but dont remember choosin did like the rest just the same dont know why went to the university cant understand it some kind of robot dont know why im doin anything tryin to find the truth of things seem to grasp it must be no truth do what you want thats truth got no standards any more things used to be good bad cool uncool now its all the same kill steal rape whats the difference no reason not to do anything like stavrogin lost distinction between good and evil lost touch with my people always feelin outside tryin so hard to get in maybe ought to stay outside become a hermit go into the desert climb to the mountain top ive seen it now i see where i was where i wasnt cant go back cant go back to a lie gotta go somewhere gotta find somethin so difficult with people everybodys so screwed up talkin seems so futile cant seem to communicate is it me or them so many barriers prejudices just wanna play wanna have fun everybodys so serious makin me serious must be someone like me somewhere there arent any means cause there arent any ends i know it theres just now got to stop dreamin get to work cant seem to get up in the morning what a life somethin holdin me down dont know what a weight on my chest pain inside gotta fight it but too weak worlds so dark wanna die leave me be all this noise traffic horns screeching shouting all this commotion and me alone in a crowded room whered everybody go everybodys doin somethin but me seems everyones got a goal doctor lawyer indian chief some sort of job how do they choose wanna know four walls and a book always must be somethin else sick of being alone gotta find someone dont understand it going crazy worlds changin before my eyes like i never saw nothin before now hearin myself talk seein myself act is that me whom i tryin to impress seems when i talk i lie never say what i want like i want cant talk to people like that must be a short circuit between the mouth and the brain listenin to what im sayin hearin the lie stutterin thinkin others must see the act the lie words so useless success must be who can tell the biggest lie feel like a window people lookin through me what am i what i think i am you are what you think you are what you eat or what others see me as everybodys wearin masks personalities egos personas lies illusion maya nothins real any more nothins like it used to be lookin at things seein what they are really are really saw jill through her hand not even the palm read her right through her hand her fear her maleness whod believe me felt so embarrassed seein her secrets had to leave whod believe me and then that feelin comin on no drugs nothin just somethin from within surgin into my brain electric current worlds so fine so beautiful every thin sparklin dogshit like chocolate streets strewn with diamonds and lace euphoria for me everywhere paradise on earth and im supposed to get a job jesus h christ a whole world goin on inside me and people just seein me comin and goin comin and goin must be some reason for being here never asked to come here be born what am i supposed to do cant seem to find an answer cant believe im supposed to work forty years and die gotta be somethin else gotta create illusions to do somethin dreams truth of absurdity leads to inaction put some sort of circle round me despair flowin outta my skin no maybe let it go all the way dissolve completely then through an act of will create myself superman sometimes feel so alone have a woman that is a comfort but comfort only gotta keep going cant give up make the whole world my comfort why not reasoning things never works warps the mind gotta feel my way through rather feel somethin than understand it dont know how i ended up where i am must be a key some-where just gotta put the pieces together find out must be some relationships interrelationships somewhere break with the past start all over a leap into the unknown ha such pride didnt know what i was doing may never know again follyfuck the past follyfuck the future only the present now now now i can do anything im master of the world im god master of the world ha so trite slave to my freedom feel like a pendulum slowing back and forth up and down panic and despair gettin tired already come someone julie feel me stroke me tell me what i write is good tell me please it is worthwhile tell me please its nothing less than poetry inspired flowing words tell me tell me please tell me that you love me in the gutter noisy machines rolling past left behind again getting dirty afraid of the dark quick lock the doors jump into bed afraid alone so to sleep quickly find someone pass the test get an A why am i alone how smart to get an A not those horrible Ds and Fs D is for dirty F is for filthy you know A is for antiseptic accomplishment oh how smart i am whenever sad look at little cards with As on them i am an A person much better than D or F persons who are bad people dark and dirty who dont succeed look i tell you there are the gogetters and donothings just walk on the clean right light mind side not the dirty wild dark body side dont hang around with the wrong people marry rich have children get settled in a good profession fraternities universities why teach i suppose but lies and nonsense but if i was offered something wed in a wedding i do what priest without a religion nice sermon darling all our friends said so where is everybody hundred joined us in holy wedlock havent seen em since do you think love is fear do you think solitude is sin oh my god pardon me for i have swept floors perhaps a child will understand me julie why are you there and me here why why what happened tell me please i want to got to know cant remember anything anymore cant remember anything cant remember cant remember anything cant remember cant remember remember remember remember remember....what?

BYE, BYE, DR. SELTZER

Today, a day off from work, must be a great day I think to myself, for today I've received a letter. It's the first letter I've received in six months besides the telephone and electric bills. I decide to savor the moment, not to open it until after breakfast, just let it lay there next to the soggy cheerios and burnt toast. I keep looking at it: it's from a small college in San Francisco. Why would a college write me? Why would anyone write me? After gulping what is left of my instant coffee, I open it gingerly, carefully, as if it were a precious love letter from one of my many mistresses I don't have.

> *Dear Mr. Allswang, in response to your application, you have been chosen to be interviewed for the position of lecturer in political science. Please report to Buccal Hall, Room 4768 at the date and time specified below.*

Application? What application? Oh, yes, about a year ago, sending out those letters to all those colleges. Just got married and desperate for a job. Yes, I remember, how I hated doing it, the niche of any sort of career disgusting me.

The date is for two weeks hence, a period of intense anxiety. As each day goes by the interview takes on more and more importance. I can't understand it. It's as if my whole life depends on this little interview, and I can't decide whether to go or not. I suppose the anxiety would go away if I could just make a real decision. But I can't. Something deeper in me that

I'm not aware of is pulling me apart. The only thing I know is this knot in my stomach. I don't think I've eaten more than a couple of yogurts and a banana the whole two weeks. As the day approaches the anxiety gets so bad that I can't go to work. Yet it's impossible for me to sit in my chair thinking or reading. George, working and carousing, is never around to talk or joke with so I can forget myself. The other two or three people I know are not available either. I go to a couple of movies, some comedies, for distraction. The contrast just makes me feel more miserable. I hear a chorus of voices inside screaming at me, closing in on me. Everything is a jumble. Can't make it out. What are you saying?! What do you want from me?! They won't go away. I wake up and there they are, gargoyles and basilisks, growling and shouting at me in this strange language that makes no sense, violent gibberish from a hostile land. The only thing to do keep moving. I pull on the clothes scattered over the floor and start to walk. For some strange reason I'm afraid to go outside, afraid someone will see my fear, afraid of being afraid. I walk in circles in the decrepit room, fragments of shouts and scraps of thought filling my brain. The walls begin to close in, like a mainspring, tighter and tighter. I'm alone and I'm panic stricken. I bolt. I walk the pavement like a maniac all day long. I walk my body a twisted rope, my shoulders touch my ears. I can hardly breathe. I walk up and down the hills of the City, Land's End to Fisherman's Wharf, downtown to the Outer Mission. I see nothing. I hear nothing. Only the knot, the voices, the tattered thought, a thousand contradictions....

When the day comes for the interview I'm in pretty bad shape. I can't really say I've decided to go because there is simply no one to decide, but still, some semblance of a personality, as if in a trance, does the necessary to dust off a suit that's about five years out of style and get my body to the college. It feels like a thirteen-year-old girl about to go to her first prom, especially when I see its hand aflutter asking George to fix its tie.

"Don't worry," he says upon leaving for work, "just tell them what they want to hear. You'll get the job."

I grab a bus weak-kneed and lily-livered. 'Tell them what they want to hear,' I say to myself falling into a seat. Goddamn I'm so sick of telling people what they want to hear. George, he says that so easily, just lie he says, second-nature to him, isn't it? Just tell them what they want to hear. Everybody, everywhere, lies and more lies. Pick up a newspaper—lies. Overhear a conversation—lies. Turn on the TV—there's one of our so-called leaders giving a speech, some fat politician dishing out lies like pork barrels. Now wait a minute, everybody couldn't be willingly telling lies. No, the human race may be a lost cause, but it can't be that perfidious. Maybe everybody thinks they're telling the truth and don't even know they're telling lies. Could that be? And do I lie and don't know it? But how can you lie and not know it? But it is true, isn't it? I'm always lying, always defending myself, saying things I don't know anything about, supporting a position I've taken, or an action, not really knowing why I do anything at all.

When I was in the National Guard, for example, called up to go to Watts in L.A., blacks were burning down half the city. They wanted me to help stop them! Gave me a loaded rifle and said, "If they try to get past you, shoot." But I was all for it. Burn the damn city, burn it all down! Brought over as slaves and treated that way ever since. What stake did they have in the game, except to spend the little money they had on the useless tinsel the society poured out. Yeah, burn it down, why not? Sack it! Loot it! What's it all worth anyway, a society with twenty-three brands of laundry detergent, all pure white. The riots must've really pissed 'em off in the valley. All the TV stations carried it. 'Goddamn niggers,' I can hear 'em say, 'now there's no Gunsmoke and what'll the kids do without Lassie. Look at the ashes in the pool, Henry. Damn niggers!'

But did I go? Yeah, I went. Sure I did. Couldn't say no, but never decided a thing. Just got carried along. Hey, it's just like now, isn't it? Going to this stupid interview. When's this all gonna stop. When am I gonna start doing what I think. It was so insane, too, all these pot-bellied clerks and fat-ass truck drivers, all playing war, itching to squeeze the trigger, 'kill a few niggers' in the name of 'order,' 'private property,' and our glorious nation built on rivers of blood. Lies and more lies. Just a bit of excitement in their hopelessly idiotic lives. Something to talk about at Jack's Bar on Saturday night.

I remember leaving the armory in the truck, remember saying to myself: 'What are you doing here, you idiot? You might be killed for something you don't even believe in.' Remember being scared shitless, too. Then we're pulling out and a guy pulls up in a white Mercedes shouting 'get the niggers!' So pissed off, I pull up my M-1; and slowly, deliberately, get the fucker in a good steady bead. Don't know what might have happened if the truck hadn't swerved and I lost my balance....

Traveling through Watts, looks-like it's been napalmed. Fire, smoke, sirens, burnt out buildings everywhere. Groups of blacks standing 'round, feelin' damn proud of themselves. So what if they have to go back and live in the ruins. The lie's been exposed, hasn't it? Nowhere now for the rats to hide. Get dropped off in some part of the ghetto that's been thoroughly burned out and ransacked. Feel the shiver up my spine seeing the flames licking up the few last timbers of a house and all the streetlights shot out, and the feeling it's all a game as we hug the wall going up the street. Not a black in sight. Then real bullets start ricocheting over our heads. We hit the deck. Turns out it's another squad across the street. Took us for snipers. Imagine dying like that 'cause some fool playing soldier was given a loaded rifle. I'm given a roadblock to man. Lucky nobody came at me—probably would've been riddled before I decided to shoot. About midnight hear machine gun fire a block away. Couldn't believe it; turned out was just a family who panicked at the roadblock. Poor bastard must've hit the gas instead of the brakes. Whole family wiped out. And then, yes, those bastards, the guy who did it got a medal! Boy, was he proud! And all the rest of 'em with their stupid little ribbon on their uniforms....And all I had to do was say no, I don't want any part of your bullshit and be ready to accept the consequences....And then afterwards, talkin' to my brother-in-law explaining in the most perfectly logical-rational-systematical-philosophical manner my reasons for joining in the insanity, having to do with responsibility, duty, morality and other such crap. Lies, all lies that I made myself believe.

My God, I really do live backwards. I find myself doing something, and hell if I know why, and then create reasons for having done it. Should be the other way around, no? But damn if I can find a reason for doing anything. Must be why I spend half my life in my chair. But why do I have to defend myself? What am I afraid of? Who gives a damn? Wait a minute, of course, I lie to others in order to lie to myself. I'd think myself crazy if I didn't create reasons for my actions, create a reasonable little world for myself. But I don't have any reasons really. Maybe I am crazy—or is everyone like that? Then everyone's crazy. But who would admit it? No, if you asked somebody they would very logically give you a reason for their actions, and it would sound very right, too. But it couldn't be true, could it? There can't be any reason for doing anything, only a rationalization, a justification, a lie, to support a belief, a phony thought-world. Things really seem to just happen. The most you could say truthfully would be 'I don't know,' or 'I can't help myself,' or 'I just have to,' or something like that. Yes, that would be the truth. But what a truth! How can I live in a world like that? Oughta blow my brains out, sick of lying....

The bus hits a pothole shaking me out of my thought. I look out the window and become fascinated by the Victorian houses going by. This one, with the turret, a chateau out of Stendhal. And that one, with the curlicues carved over the porch, like a funhouse at Ocean Park. Ah ha, grinning at me, the huge bay window, and the two squinty eyes in the roof....Wait a minute, this interview, I've got to get my thoughts together. What are they going to ask me? What'll they want to know?—What's the difference? I don't remember a damn thing. Why? Why? Why did I read all those books? Why did I take all those courses? It was just a year ago, and now it doesn't mean a thing. I got a master's degree and that doesn't mean a thing either. Just a piece of paper with fancy letters on it. But they're gonna ask me things! I won't know what to say! I'm gonna have to lie! My mind's a blank. Master of Arts, my ass! Master of nothing! Nothing left, all wiped out, erased, erased like a blackboard, *tabula rasa.*

I'm completely surprised by the man falling against me as the bus makes a sharp turn.

"Excuse me," he says, "I'm so sorry. I wasn't prepared for the turn."

He looks so apologetic and serious, and me, I'm so far away. I just stare and then start laughing like a hyena. It's just too incongruous. A jackhammer up my backbone wouldn't faze me now. Poor guy thinks I'm nuts. But this interview! There must be something I remember. Let me see. Hobbes's *Leviathan,* something about life being brutish and short. Rousseau and the

Social Contract. Nothing, a complete blank. However, in the *Confessions* I do remember him getting a sensual pleasure by being beaten by the pastor's daughter. I can just see it now: 'Mr. Allswang, could you expound for us now on the thought of Jean-Jacques Rousseau?' 'Well, no, not really, but I can tell you how got his jollies.' No wonder I don't know anything, that crazy Prof Himmendorf I took so many courses from. All he thought about was Freud. I even psychoanalyzed *Antigone* for him once in one of my papers. Thought he'd like that. Incredible the way he'd stop in the middle of a sentence, tilt his head to the left, stick his finger in his ear and ask himself out loud why he just made that slip of the tongue. Or the old fogy Finster reading his notes day after day. Glad I found the book he copied word for word—never had to go to class. So many books, so many names: Plato's *Republic* and St. Augustine's *City of God*, Machiavelli's *The Prince*, Burke's *Reflections on the Revolution in France*, Mill's *On Liberty*, Marx's *Capital*. Who else? Hegel, Thomas More, Sorel's *Reflections on Violence*, I liked that I remember. No end to it all. Who was it spending all those hours in the library under neon lights, reading to the rhythm of the air conditioner, huddled away in a corner memorizing facts and ideas, writing papers?

Writing papers! What an adept I became at that! Especially the stews worth four stars in the Michelin Guide. A pinch of this writer, a dash of that one, a teaspoon of this theory, a cup of the other, all properly steamed through with footnotes for every sentence. All they wanted to read was something logical and well substantiated. Didn't matter at all what I wrote about as long as it was 'consistent' and the bibliography thick and well-typed. Yes, indeedy, I became a real *cordon bleu*. Didn't give a damn what I wrote as long as it looked good and was sugary to the palate, cotton candy stuff. At times I got this sickness, intellectual fits, called in academia "Having-an-idea-of-your-own." They always caught me, though. Whenever I dared to slip one of these "ideas-of-my-own" into the concoction, it was like putting in too much pepper. Amidst sneezing and coughing they would bring out their thick red pencils and put down things in the margin like "substantiate!," "quote?", "reference?" One attempt at revolt took place when I had an idea I really liked, that I thought would be really appreciated for its originality and subtle understanding of the problem, and all I got back was the usual "cite evidence" in red pencil. So pissed I was, I bought a pencil in phosphorescent orange and printed in large unmistakable letters: "THE EVIDENCE IS TO BE FOUND IN MY OWN MIND" and gave the thing back to him. It came back a month later with his reply written in an almost illegible tiny script: "Maybe, but it's not scholarship." Okay, I learned to play the game. I became the best there was. It came to the point where I would take a position on a given topic depending on which books were the most available. I would even take the viewpoint opposite my own feelings if it meant I could get more citations for my bibliography. I was taught, and I did accept (for who was I to doubt it) that the truth of the question at hand depends solely on the number of citations, that the more references I had the truer the position I took.

Now it seems so ridiculous, but something in me must have liked it: handling, fondling, playing with ideas. In some strange way I thought I would come to the truth and that when I did I could decide something, what to do, how to live. Never found the truth, did I? How could I have been so naive? All these theories I don't even remember, just theories written after the fact to justify or attack the present condition. Then what is the present condition if not based on a theory. It just is, yes, that's it, it just is, following from what preceded, following some law of development of its own. Then why are all these books seen as so important? The glorious French Revolution and the great American democracy, all bathed in the blood of the Temple of Reason, supposedly based on the thought of Rousseau, a pathological pervert. But things just go on. Marx, Lenin, Stalin, Mao, socialism, communism, just people and ideas justifying and attacking, trying to make sense out of the world. But the Vedas said it long ago, didn't they? In the last cycle at the end of an age, in the last era of the *Kali-Yuga,* the lowest class takes control before the final catastrophe. Why not let things be, let people be. It'll happen anyway. Nations, peoples, civilizations—huge worlds rolling through time and one little man looks around and doesn't like what he sees. So he goes into the British Museum and writes a theory on society. And every man who has a grudge takes it up and starts to kill all those who don't fit into the revolution to come. ("All those wearing glasses were executed as decadent bourgeois.") And if it doesn't fit into the theory, well then it just doesn't exist, does it? Things like grass, stars, and consciousness. The conflict isn't between capitalism and communism, representative democracy and the dictatorship of the proletariat. It's all the same thing. West and East now, they're both based on ideas, ideas arising out of the demented reason of some misfit or other. West and East: where everybody is supposed to live by an idea that may have nothing at all to do with what they are. The alienation of man: people trying to fit and squeeze and pummel their life into an idea that came from outside of them, that they never came to from their own experience, but from a book, or more insidiously in the schools, or more directly, hammered in by mama and papa. Our society is unnatural because instead of growing and developing on its own like a flower with people naturally finding their place depending on what they are, what they've been born with, doing what they're cut out for, what they like, ruled by natural rulers, everything and everybody is layered over by the cement of ideas to which everyone is supposed to conform, the first and worst being that everyone is essentially the same and therefore should have an equal say in every decision—which is a lie to begin with and impossible in practice and therefore leads to the opposite, with power in the hands of the least capable and the exploitation of the rest. Wait a minute, hasn't that been my life up to now? Acting by ideas I never accepted, never even thought about. Just swept along like a block of driftwood, never asking why, always making sure my name is spelled right on the computer cards. No wonder I don't remember anything; I never really studied anything from a real question of my own. I even took courses that meant absolutely nothing to me, like accounting and journalism. Or if I did have a question it was always abstract, find a theory to live by, a philosophy to defend....What am I in this bus for, going to this interview? I don't want a job teaching political science. There's nothing to teach. It's either lies or trivia anyway. Go back to academia? The higher you go, the worse it gets. Instead of broadening your mind, you've got to specialize, narrow it down, become an 'expert' in this little world of ideas going back and forth leading nowhere...

Oughta give a course on rocks. Something useful. Go to the Mojave Desert, get a hundred or so good baked rocks, some big, some small, some round, some jagged. I'd give a course on feeling rocks. We'd all sit in a circle and pass the rocks around, feeling them, rubbing them, and the first one who said a word, we'd all let loose, stone him to death, and on his grave, on a big granite slab, with my own hands I'd chisel these words: RECEIVED AN F FOR PROSTITUTING LIFE.

Why can't I get out of the bus? I don't want to go! I don't want the goddamn job! I can't figure it out. Why can't I do what I think? Who or what is in this bus, in this body. Not me, that's for sure. Some stranger I don't know and I don't like. He doesn't do what I tell him at all. Just says and does anything he wants. Who is he? Where did he come from? What am I going to say at the interview? I can't let him say his stupidities and make a fool of me as usual. Don't remember a thing about theory. Maybe I could talk about practice, my experience in the Peace and Freedom Party, for example. It was a good idea really. Everything from the bottom up, local clubs and all that. Yes, very nice indeed until the infighting started, the intrigues, the grab for power. Why does everything start so pure and then go right downhill? Can't understand it, people take the organization for the ideal which the organization was meant to serve. Of course, people can't admit that, no, that all they want is power in the organization. So we get lies and more lies. And me, was I any different? I found my little niche; I became an expert in migratory farm workers. Did a lot of research and killed two birds with one stone: a report for a sociology class and a position paper for the party. Wasn't that clever! Me, an expert. What a joke! Never even been on a farm, let alone talk to a farm worker. Just read a few books and articles, put together what others wrote, made it sound convincing, and presto! I'm an expert—plus a good grade in sociology. From that, got myself elected as delegate to the founding convention. Pretty smooth, *n'est-ce pas?* What did I care about migratory farm workers? Not a damn thing! How could I if I never even met one?! Yet, I made myself believe I cared. I know I did. I lied, first to myself, then to everyone else. I had all the answers and really didn't know a thing. All a bluff and I didn't even know it was a bluff. I believed it. A real intellectual radical I was. A demonstration here, a march there, a meeting now and then or an angry letter against the War. Why? Why? I really didn't give a damn. But everybody around me was taking a stand, weren't they? When everybody's talking politics, you've got to have something to say, don't you? So I found a position, too, a very reasoned well-thought-out position, that having said often enough I began to believe. Suppose I could have taken the opposite viewpoint just as well. Just that something was eating me up inside. Was against everything. But it was all ideas, just thoughts turning round. Then I felt guilty for not acting on the thoughts and ideas I took up to have something to say, and so put the ideas into action by engaging in political acts. No wonder I never really felt committed. It was all a lie! It wasn't real! I didn't really live what I was talking about. Every time I said a word, it was a lie. Every act I made was unreal. They had to be because they were based only on thought, but I didn't know it, because I had to lie to myself first. Why did I lie to myself? Because I had to create a world for myself, that phony thought-world to hide...to hide what? My God! Yes, of course, *to hide the fact that I don't exist!.* Don't need to read huge tomes to know what nothingness is: *Being and Nothingness.* Just look into myself. What do I see? Nothing. Lies and thoughts, that's all. A shell of lies and thoughts, and life just bounces off. No wonder I'm always bored, why everything is so dead. Nothing can reach me through this armor of thought. Sensation, feeling, experience, filtered through my ideas, my thought, my lies. Is it just me? Does everybody live like this? Is everybody in this bus living right now this lie? Is it true, in fact, that no one really exists?! ...Existence ...Being... What does it mean to be?... Meursault... Why did Camus' book *The Stranger* affect me so and Sartre's *Nausea* and Beckett's *Waiting for Godot.* As if I was missing something...But what? Life maybe. This contradiction between thought and life. Then what's the mind for? Maybe just to take part in the world, read maps, count change, not create a make-believe world, castles in the sky, dreams....'It was better to burn than to disappear,' Meursault said. Why does this phrase keep bubbling up into my brain over and over? What did he mean, 'disappear'? Of course, disappear into thought, theories, dreams, daydreams. ...which is not to be... To be! To be!... Face to face. ...

Okay, okay, now stop, Michael. You're going to an interview! You're going to an interview for a job, a job as a teacher. I can't talk about my political experiences. They were all lies. They'll know they're lies even if I did take part, even if they don't know they know they'll know. People can tell these things. You can't hide a lie. Even when you think you're telling the truth, and the other thinks you are telling the truth, he still knows you're lying, even if he doesn't believe he knows. But why is it a lie if, in fact, I did have the experience? Because I didn't do it for itself. I did it to satisfy a lie I told myself about what it was, to give myself a life. But a life based on thought is not a life. It's why Nietzsche went mad. It's why Rimbaud gave up poetry to run guns. It's why Van Gogh plugged himself in the gut. Why do I feel like a brother to these men, these men who suffered and died a tortured and twisted life. I, too, could have written a *Season in Hell*, letters like Van Gogh's. I probably would have already written *Zarathustra* if I just had some Alps. California, it's too hot and easy and crazy, too dispersed. Everything here's on the same level, the bottom one. How to rise up out of the morass? Gotta get outta here! I know, I'll go to Paris and write my *Tropic of Cancer*. Oh, this is so trite, so romantic. Henry Miller himself said somewhere that the real artist is he who has conquered the romantic in himself. But then there's Dostoyevsky, and what else is there to say? He said it all; from the basement to the attic, there isn't a corner of the human mind that he didn't investigate. *Notes from the Underground*, that's my book, that's me! Why didn't I write it? Why can't I decide anything? Because the moment I have a desire to act, at the same time I see the uselessness of it. Oh, it's so trite, this Hamlet type, the pale cast of thought and all that. But what am I supposed to do? Close my eyes and walk into a wall? It's absurd, yes, life is absurd. Everything's been said.

To act you have to stop thinking. That's what people do, don't they? Attach themselves to things, causes, people, jobs, create an identity for themselves, an idea of themselves, that allows them to act. Why I can't do that I haven't the foggiest. The eternal 'Why?' and 'What for?' the moment I have a desire. A psychological quirk from childhood no doubt. But then everybody must be like that, only they find a way to cover it over by a lie called 'father,' 'lawyer,' 'writer,' 'wife,' etc. But it is a good question, isn't it? 'Why? What for?' I mean if you're at all interested in the truth. But you carry any thought back far enough, it dissolves into absurdity and nonsense. So I sit in my chair until I can't stand it anymore and then run out and make a fool of myself, forcing myself on people, so desirous of getting out of my thought. It takes me a month in my chair just getting over the shame and embarrassment of what I said and did. Then the thinking again....the leap into life...over and over...so true and so trite...I don't even know if I would live like this if I hadn't read Dostoyevsky....What am I if not a caricature of a character in a book, a lie of a lie....

Oh, my God! I'm almost there. What does all this have to do with what I'm going to say to the judges? A few people are going to ask me some questions. If I happen to come up with the right answers my whole life might change. I might become a respected member of society, a good academic, a professor! I might even write an interesting book on the philosophy of Nietzsche, a brilliant compendium of existentialism, a history of the whole Western philosophical tradition from my own particular point of view. Who knows, I might start an intellectual movement; people will come to my door asking me for advice on deep, personal questions about the nature of Man and the Cosmos. I will be asked to sign moral manifestos. I will be invited to the White House and the President will ask me to counsel him as to the moral consequences of his next war. I will be asked to speak before the United Nations. Because of my wisdom and superhuman understanding I will be given leadership over the whole planet! Or else, if I pop out with some usual stupidity, I will be given a condescending smile and sent back to the bakery and my chair, a worm rotting away, sinking, thinking, 'now if only I had said...' But it really makes no difference what I do. How can it, when it's just a matter of convention, a question of social status? If I don't define myself by my social position, I still am, aren't I? I'm still here. I'm still a human being. Like animal being, tree being...being...strange word...a kid, I used to think it was 'bean,' 'human bean.' What the hell is 'being' anyway? And why don't I feel what I think? If it doesn't make any difference, why do I care so much about this interview? Funny that, my thoughts seem to have no bearing at all on how I feel, on what I do....*There's something definitely wrong here!*

Now obviously I need to act more and think less. Stop reading Sartre and Freud and Jung and Laing. All this psychology. I've gone through my whole life a thousand times, each from a different psychological point of view. It doesn't change a thing. I need something new, but what? I need a reason to act, first of all. Maybe that's the whole problem. I keep looking for an idea on which to base my actions, I want to *choose* my life, I want to *control* everything. I want to be sure! And why? Because I'm afraid of the unknown, I'm afraid of letting my life happen, of allowing myself to be what I am. Yes, somehow I've got to get beyond all this psychology. Dostoyevsky is not the answer. He's John the Baptist crying in the wilderness. He keeps talking about consciousness, consciousness in terms of knowing, of knowing more about oneself psychologically. He must be wrong here. What he's talking about is being more intelligent, more insightful, more perceptive, using your mind, intellectual masturbation. It has nothing to do with consciousness. In fact, the collection of knowledge gives the illusion of more consciousness, when the truth is that if I read every book ever written, underlining the important passages, and making marginal notes to myself, I wouldn't be the slightest bit more conscious. Actually, because I thought I was getting to the Truth, I would never search for the Way to it, nor ever have the *experience* of it. Having more consciousness must not be *learning* more, but *acting* more within and without, *being* more in myself and in the world. Rimbaud, Nietzsche, Van Gogh, Kierkegaard are martyrs then of a New Age. They took their lives to the outer limits and so knew the truth of the human condition. They saw themselves at low tide floundering on the beach of absurdity rotting away with the lifeless seaweed and the desolate rocks, desperately lapping up the few trickles that came their way: a poem, an insight, a well-turned phrase, a painting. They went mad, they killed themselves, they got cancer. Why? Because they were true to their vision and did not want to compromise with the truth. They did not want, they could not, take part in the social lie—and thus artists are born, and vagabonds, and neurotics and every form of madness. In the end, this is my choice: a respectable liar or a half-mad artist. What a choice! No wonder I've been so anxious about this interview; it's what it represents. I would be stupid having studied the lives of these men, these martyrs, only to make the same mistake. It's the *pride* that's got to go, the *pride*, the belief that one is superior. But like them I cannot, even if I am going to this interview, take part in the Lie. Now that I've seen it, there's no going back. Even though the world has become a vast empty space filled with things and beings aimlessly roving over the wasted land, and however much I want to take my place and be loved and respected and use my talents for the common good, be appreciated by my fellow man, it would never work. They'd find me out eventually. Little things would tip them off. Like not laughing at the boss's jokes, not knowing who won the World Series, or even who was playing. Not caring about promotions. Little things, like not attending office parties, would set me off. I'd be ostracized, labeled an asocial neurotic. I wouldn't be able to stand it. I want to be loved and respected. At least if I stay in my chair, I don't know if I'm loved and respected or not. I can always hope and there's always tomorrow.

Another five minutes and I'll be there. Why don't I just go home? No, that would be cowardly, besides if anybody asks what I'm doing these days I can truthfully say I'm looking for a job teaching, and that's better than saying I'm a baker's helper. There must be another choice, another way between lying and madness. There must be somewhere someone else who came to the same contradiction and found something else. Is it the other Self? Is it the Witness? Why should you have to be neurotic to be a creator anyway? I don't see the point. I remember that party I went to last year. Everybody was fawning over this writer. He had already published five or six books, but he was drunk and couldn't walk. He kept talking about himself. He looked a wreck. They had to carry him home. If that's what you have to be like to be an artist, what's the point? I'm a man first, aren't I? I'm a human being. What I do should help me be. In accomplishing my work, I become what I really am. My work should be a means and not an end, a means of becoming myself. I've got to do *something* in the real world. Why not do what I like? If I know that one's social position doesn't mean a damn thing, why am I so ashamed of myself? Why do I blush when I say I work in a bakery? Why do I always feel I ought to be doing other than what I do? Why am I always guilty without ever being judged? Why am I never at peace? Why? Why?

When I enter the building I still have no idea what I am going to say. I'm nervous, a little sweaty, but not overly so. All the thought on the way here has drained me. Nothing has been resolved. I only know that I definitely don't want to be here, but somehow I feel obligated to see it through, though to whom or to what I'm obligated is still a mystery. The secretary asks me my name. I tell her, and she says, yes, they were expecting me. She tells me to follow her through a door into the next room. She points to a chair at the bottom end of tables formed in the shape of a T and asks me to be seated. I thank her and do so. At the other end facing me are three men. One of them begins to speak:

"Well, Mr. Allswang, we're glad you could make it. Please make yourself at ease. Of course, you know we are looking to hire, on a part-time basis only, a lecturer in both the American political system and in the Western tradition of political philosophy. This interview is to help us gauge, along with your written application, your particular qualifications for this position. Just for your information, we are interviewing fifteen out of the roughly three hundred applications received, about five percent. My name is Dr. Seltzer, and I am chairman of the department. On my right is Dr. Johnson of the Faculty Recruitment Committee, and on my left is Mr. Casterman, representing the Graduate Student Advisory Body. I believe Dr. Johnson would like to start off the questioning. Is that all right, Bob?"

"Yes, of course, Jim. Well now, Mr. Allswang, in looking over your application it says that since you left graduate school you had been working for the U. S. Post Office as a mailman. Is that still the case?"

"You have to understand. I was married at the time. I had to get a job. We didn't have any money. So, yes, yes, I was a postman for about a year, I guess it was, but I quit after the strike. It got too uncomfortable."

"The strike?"

"Yes, you remember, the wildcat in Oakland in support of the New York walkout. Twenty of us closed down the whole Oakland Post Office. Nobody would cross our picket lines. I wasn't the initiator you understand, but it seemed like the right thing to do at the time. Anyway, the union busted the strike and after that I started getting harassed, so I quit. I got a job a few months ago working in a bakery."

"Hmmm. Yes, I understand. It's difficult finding teaching jobs these days, but tell me, have you engaged in any other, uh, political activities in the past?"

"Well, yes, at the university I was involved in some student strikes in a rather minor way, but I did take an active part in the Peace and Freedom Party."

"The Peace and Freedom Party? If I remember correctly, they were associated with the Black Panthers, isn't that right?"

"Well, as far as I can recall, there was some talk of collaboration at the founding convention, but I really don't know what came of it. I had to drop all that when I went back East to graduate school."

"Have you been involved in any other, shall we say, left-leaning organizations?"

"Left-leaning organizations? Oh...no, no, of course not."

"Now, you just said you were married at the time. What is your marital situation at present?"

"Uh, yes, well, I'm divorced now. My wife left me."

"That's all right, we don't need the details, you know. We just want to get a general picture of your situation."

"Yes, I'm just trying to be helpful."

"Mr. Casterman, would you like to ask Mr. Allswang some questions?"

"Yes, I would, Dr. Seltzer. It's obvious from your application, Mr. Allswang, that your main interest has been in political philosophy and political theory, so it would probably be best if we concentrate on that. Now, could you please give us, just in your own words, a brief summary of the thought of Thomas Paine."

"Thomas Paine, the American?"

"Yes, that's the only one I know."

"Of course, well, uh, Tom Paine was one of those thinkers who, uh, through his pamphlets and tracts, helped foment the American Revolution. Essentially, he was for liberty and justice, following undoubtedly from the French tradition of Rousseau and Montesquieu."

"Well, that hardly gets to the heart of the matter, Mr. Allswang. I mean you can agree that everyone is for liberty and justice...."

"Yes, you understand, it's been a long time since I read Thomas Paine. I'm sure if I just went over my textbooks it would all come back, but at the moment, I'm afraid...."

"Of course, of course, we understand, you've been away from academia for a while...."

"Yes, that's right, thank you."

"The other course to be taught is on the American political system, so perhaps a more general question would give you more leeway in showing us the extent of your knowledge. With this in mind, perhaps you could, just again in a general way, give us what you see as the philosophical and theoretical basis of the American political system."

"Yes, the philosophical and theoretical basis of the American political system...umm, if you'll just give me a minute to collect my thoughts..."

"Of course, take your time."

A heavy silence ensues. I become aware of the clickety-clack of a typewriter in the outer room. The buzz from the neon lights which I have not heard at all, now is as insistent as a mosquito. My mind is a complete blank. I have no idea what to say. They just sit and look at me expectantly. The moment of truth. My future depends on what comes out of my mouth in the next instant. I feel the blood rising into my face and the sweat sticky in my armpits. I loosen my tie automatically and cough. Nobody says a word. Then something very strange happens. I have the distinct impression of being outside my body. I say outside even though I never felt that I had left it. I just never noticed or thought about it. But I must have because the impression is of being outside. At the same time, I see myself as being flooded with fear, as being fear. My thoughts, my emotions, the tension all over my body are seen as all conditioned by this fear. I become acutely aware for the first time of my brow knotted up like rope and my right foot tapping incessantly. Where my thoughts should have been, I notice just a sort of dull roaring. I feel I am going to explode when a sharp buzzer sounds somewhere in the building sending a shiver up and down my spine. Then, by itself, my body begins to relax. I feel a sensation flowing in my body as though I am coming back inside. I feel my brow unwind, my shoulders drop, my foot stop tapping. I begin to feel myself sitting with my buttocks spread over the seat of the chair and my vertebrae up against the back of it. Simultaneously, I begin to see the room as if for the first time, as if a fairy caused it magically to appear with a wave of her wand. It seems to me totally inhuman: the four walls are completely bare and coated with this sparkling plaster you find in cheap motel rooms. The ceiling is made simply of white insulating tiles, while the floor is linoleum having a banal design of black and white squares. The one large window has an institutional venetian blind that is open, putting the three men in stark relief. The tables are of the folding type, with false-grained formica tops. For some reason, I can look at the three men in the eye, and what I see horrifies me. All these impressions are taking place in the space of a few seconds. A change in posture is all that can be noticed by the three men waiting for their answer, for I am definitely aware that I am sitting up straighter in my chair.

What horrifies me is that I see these men as not really being themselves. All three of them are double. They are double because of me. They are playing the roles of judges, but they don't know it. I feel horribly guilty and embarrassed at seeing this. I want to run away. I feel caught in a horrible contradiction. I see the fear in their own faces. The young Mr. Casterman, I feel like telling him not worry, that people do respect him for his intellect; that one day, he too will be a full professor. Just stay in there, kid. And Dr. Johnson looks like a little pup who lost his mother. Why is he hiding it? And Seltzer seems as though all he wants to do is please somebody, probably his old man. Those are the three people I want to talk to, but I know I can't. They'd think I was nuts. They'd put me away. They wouldn't understand. It's all a horrible lie. It wouldn't be so bad if they knew they were just playing this role of judge and they knew that I knew, then we could communicate somehow on another level, no matter what was said. But they don't know. They believe they are what is only their role. I have to pretend I don't see them for what they are, I have to pretend to believe in this false situation. I have to talk to their false selves as if they were real. I can't stand it. I'm ashamed for them, embarrassed for them. Who am I to see this? And maybe it's not true at all. Maybe it's just delusions of grandeur: they're judging me, so I'll judge them. Maybe I'm just crazy. After all, I've never read anything about people actually seeing this. I've only read psychological theories about it, analyses. What can I do? How am I supposed to act? Which self should I talk to? I could pretend nobody's there maybe, and just talk, whatever comes to mind—but I'm just so sick of lying....Oh, what the hell!

"Mr. Casterman is it? Yes, to answer your question, I don't think there is any theoretical or philosophical base to the American political system. You raise your eyebrows, that surprises you. But that's exactly what I think. The American Constitution, the Declaration of Independence, the separation of powers, the social contract, of the people, by the people, for the people, etc., etc.—it's all rationalization, justification, and lies. Justification for what you ask. Well, I'll tell you. To justify and 'make legal' the birth of a country born in a river of blood, Indian blood. What really matters is who occupies the land, right? Before our great founding fathers, with their cherry trees and slaves, came over and wrote up these so-called historic documents, this land was occupied by a people, a civilization. We slaughtered them. We made Cortez look like a saint, Pizarro an angel. Of course, they probably did the same to some civilization before them. I'm not so naive as all that. Mao's right: power comes out of the barrel of a gun, or the tip of an arrow in the latter case. But let's be honest about it at least—no more lies, dissimulation, manipulation. It's not the law that rules here; it's not democracy (whatever that means these days), it's the police and the army and it's always the police and the army. Any political system is a means for those who have the power to keep it, and that's as far as it goes. The game's rigged from the beginning. Free speech is for those who have nothing to say. The moment someone or some group really begins to make headway in changing things, they're spied upon, harassed, killed in their beds. You see, I don't give a damn about your stupid job, because if I took it, I'd have to dissimulate, carry forward the social lie, cramming it into virgin minds, into youngsters ready to lap it up because they don't know any better. I voted once just for the experience and never have since. There's no choice here, none at all. Republicans, Democrats, you call that a choice. Even if there was a choice, there wouldn't be a choice. Do you understand me? It's incredible to me why anybody votes here, candidates created by publicity men, computer experts and opinion polls, everybody saying what they expect this or that group wants to hear. It's all a game, a charade, and everybody plays it as if it meant something beyond the naked grab for power, glory, money, and fame. There isn't a man anywhere who says what he believes anymore, if he believes anything at all. The whole political system is set up to dupe the people into believing that they have a say in the process, when all the power is in the corporate board rooms and the Pentagon. You're beginning to look shocked, all of you. I'm a bit surprised myself that I'm saying all this. I think this is the first time in my life I've really said what I think. In this country the latest thought depends on the latest poll. This is what you call democracy, 'by the people' and 'for the people'. This, Mr. Castleman, is your philosophical basis of the American political system."

"The name is Casterman, Casterman. Well, maybe you should..."

"Go to Russia? Is that what you were about to say, Mr. Castleman, excuse me, Casterman. Or were you going to say China or Cuba? I'm under no illusion that it's any better there. In fact, I'm sure it's worse in terms of my individual freedom and belief in the social lie, though it's really just a matter of degree. There's nothing essentially different. The individual means nothing there nor here. We just pay it more lip service. I've heard people say that in Europe, in France, for example, people really have a choice between capitalism and socialism, democracy and communism. Well, let me ask you a question. What's the difference who lies to you, the oil companies and Madison Avenue and their spokesmen in Washington or the Central Committee of the state organization? I see, Dr. Seltzer, that you wish to say something, go ahead."

"I have been following your argument and it is quite cogent. I just have one question..."

"What is my solution, right? Somehow it's immoral these days to criticize anything without having a well-thought-out plan to put in its place. I don't know, Dr. Seltzer. Once I thought anarchism was the answer. You've read, I presume, Proudhon's *General Idea of the Revolution in the 19th Century*. This was my solution for some time until I realized that it was just another idea, a utopian idea of economic cooperation that didn't consider man's perfidious nature. I toyed with Kropotkin and Bakunin as well, but in the end there's something wrong with taking an idea and then trying to fit man into it. Man, it seems to me, is larger than any idea created by human thought. One forgets that man has another side to him, a spiritual nature as well, if you like. Besides, I came to realize too that taking a ready-made idea from someone else and appropriating it as my own alienated me from life. Here I was supposed to be an anarchist while I was taking money from my father, who is a businessman, and scholarships from the government, when in theory I was for the abolition of private property and elimination of the state. I didn't even see the contradiction until later. I was always trying to make my life correspond to the idea, which it didn't want to do. My ideas have to grow out of my life, my experience; otherwise, they are useless abstractions that twist life out of shape when I try to apply them. Marxism was good for Marx, a nice exercise in thought relative to the 19th century. Why try to make this a way of life for some poor peasant in Cambodia which could only be totally alien to his traditional culture. The same goes for every other sort of -ism, including capitalism. Why do people so desperately need an -ism to cling to anyway? Maybe I just belong on the moon, or on Mars or even Jupiter. Things just don't seem right to me on this planet. But maybe that's the trouble here, that everybody is looking for a solution, a way to fix things, change things, looking for new plans and schemes. Maybe we just have to understand that we can't do anything, change anything. Things are like they are because they can't be any other way. Everything is connected. If you change the smallest thing, everything has to be changed, and who has that sort of vision? We've come to the end of the road on this earth with the type of thinking that says with a little ingenuity, a lot of planning, and tremendous goodwill, things have to turn out for the best. My God, Dr. Seltzer, don't the people see the missiles poised over the city? Well, I can see it, the city, about to be vaporized. And I see Man, Dr. Seltzer, who, like the fungus, the bacteria, the lizards, the minnows, the weasels, the sparrows, the chimpanzees, and the duckbill platypuses, will once again find his community, if not by common consent, by the new tribes wandering over the earth after the apocalypse. I can see by your face that you think I have gone stark, raving mad, Dr. Seltzer. But I don't care. I'm going to tell you what I see. And what I see are the cities crumbling and the land singing with radiation. I see the sun darkened over for generations by phosphorescent clouds. I see us bargaining the destruction of New York and Chicago for Moscow and Leningrad, like a board game, doing what's logical, reasonable, and in the best interest of all concerned. If I am insane then so is the world, for I am a child of the century; and the only thing that can probably save us is for a new Messiah to appear spreading his teaching over all the earth, turning each of us round towards ourselves....What else can I say, gentlemen, except good-bye, Dr. Seltzer, good-bye and good riddance....